KEJI YINGHAN

HUYI JIAOCHENG

科技英汉互译教程

许卉艳 编著

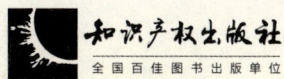
知识产权出版社
全国百佳图书出版单位

图书在版编目（CIP）数据

科技英汉互译教程/许卉艳编著. —北京：知识产权出版社，2015.9
ISBN 978 - 7 - 5130 - 3202 - 5

Ⅰ . ①科…　Ⅱ . ①许…　Ⅲ . ①科学技术—英语—翻译—高等学校—教材　Ⅳ . ①H315.9

中国版本图书馆 CIP 数据核字（2014）第 280413 号

内容提要

本教材强调理论与实践相结合，选择与时俱进的新译例、语篇及练习。各章节的内容以英汉互译的形式编排，既前后照应、相互联系，又自成一体、各有侧重。

教材内容分为两部分：第一部分是对翻译的基本知识、原则标准及常用翻译方法的介绍与实践，其中涉及选词、组句、转换、融合、分译、增译、省略、顺译、逆译等实用技巧，还包括英汉两种语言在结构及表达特点方面的详细比较，以帮助学生在翻译过程中减少母语语言文化的负迁移，并配有相关的翻译实践练习；第二部分介绍了八种科技文体的特点及翻译方法与实践，如专利、版权、合同、协议、提案、报告、科技论文及会议文件。

责任编辑：蔡　虹　　执行编辑：陈晶晶　　责任出版：孙婷婷

科技英汉互译教程

许卉艳　编著

出版发行：知识产权出版社 有限责任公司　　网　　址：http://www.ipph.cn
社　　址：北京市海淀区马甸南村 1 号　　天猫旗舰店：http://zscqcbs.tmall.com
责编电话：010 - 82000860 转 8391　　责编邮箱：shiny-chjj@163.com
发行电话：010 - 82000860 转 8101/8102　　发行传真：010 - 82000893/82005070/82000270
印　　刷：北京富生印刷厂　　经　　销：各大网上书店、新华书店及相关专业书店
开　　本：787mm ×1092mm　1/16　　印　　张：10.5
版　　次：2015 年 9 月第 1 版　　印　　次：2015 年 9 月第 1 次印刷
字　　数：290 千字　　定　　价：36.00 元
ISBN 978 - 7 - 5130 - 3202 - 5

前　言

　　《科技英汉互译教程》自 2005 年起作为中国矿业大学（北京）非英语专业研究生科技英语翻译课程的自编教材进行试用，经过近 9 年的使用、补充、修改，内容和体例得到不断的丰富和完善，融汇了笔者多年来关于翻译实践探索和研究的成果。

　　本书集英汉、汉英翻译于一体，兼顾理论性和实用性；立足于英汉语言文化差异，介绍词句和科技语篇的翻译技巧和方法；按照由词句到段篇的次序来安排教学内容，符合学生的学习规律；对常用科技文体的介绍，可帮助学生了解英汉不同语篇的写作特点和翻译技巧，提高翻译效率，胜任各类翻译工作，从而满足社会对翻译人才的实际需求。

　　本教材分翻译概要和科技文献翻译两大部分，共计 16 个单元。第一部分包括：翻译概述（如：翻译的起源、翻译历史、翻译的定义及分类、翻译的标准和过程、翻译原则、翻译与文化等）、汉英语言文化对比和各种英汉互译技巧介绍（如：选词择义，增益法，省略法，词性、句法成分和句子结构转换法，正反表达转换法，被动语态的翻译，从句和长句的翻译）。第二部分具体包括：科技文体的特点、翻译标准，以及八种科技文献的翻译，如专利、版权、合同、协议、提案、报告、科技论文及摘要、会议文件。

　　本教材的特点如下：

　　（1）系统介绍汉英语言文化对比知识，以帮助学生在翻译过程中克服母语语言文化的负迁移影响，从而形成地道、规范的目标语文本；

　　（2）词句翻译和语篇翻译相结合，对比各种不同科技语体的写作特点、翻译标准及练习范本，有助于提高学生的综合翻译能力和语篇意识；

　　（3）译例多出自笔者一手的翻译资料，内容实用多样、与时俱进，而翻译技巧的总结归纳多是笔者自己在多年的翻译实践中积累的独特翻译经验的结晶；

　　（4）汉英和英汉互译的例子放在一起编排，不但便于互相比较分析、突出翻译技巧的应用，理论密切结合实践，还可以避免重复讲解，提高学生的学习兴趣和学习效率。

　　本教材在撰写过程中参考了国内外相关书籍及文献资料，在此笔者特向相关作者表示感谢。同时还要感谢笔者所在学校中国矿业大学（北京）研究生院以及知识产权出版社编辑陈晶晶老师为本教材的顺利出版所给予的大力支持。

　　本书的读者对象为非英语专业研究生、高年级大学生和爱好翻译工作的其他外语学习者。

　　笔者水平有限，书中不当之处，望各位专家、读者不吝赐教，批评指正。

　　如有需要，可联系笔者，联系方式为：xuhuiyan1@126.com.

　　本书获中央高校基本科研业务费项目资助和中国矿业大学（北京）研究生教材及学术专著出版基金资助。

笔者于北京
2015 年 3 月 17 日

CONTENTS

Part I Translation in General
Unit 1 Introduction to Translation

1. Origin of Translation—*The Tower of Babel*

According to the *Old Testament*, after the Flood, the children of Noah had children, and their children had children. At that time, the whole earth was of one language, and of one speech. And it came to pass, as they journeyed from the east, that they found a plain in the land of Shinar, and they dwelt there. And they said one to another: "Go to, let us make brick, and burn them thoroughly." And they had brick for stone, and slime for morter. And they said: "Go to, let us build us a city and a tower, whose top may reach unto heaven; and let us make us a name, lest we be scattered abroad upon the face of the whole earth." And the Lord came down to see the city and the tower, which the children of men builded. And the Lord said: "Behold, the people is one, and they have all one language; and this is what they begin to do: and now nothing will be restrained from them, which they have imagined to do. Go to, let us go down, and there confound their language, that they may not understand one another's speech." So the Lord scattered them abroad from thence upon the face of all the earth: and they left off to build the city. Therefore is the name of it called Babel, because the Lord did there confound the language of all the earth: and from thence did the Lord scatter them abroad upon the face of all the earth (King James Version).

Since then people speak different languages and live in different parts of the world. As a result, language becomes the first barrier for them to communicate with each other, and of course they can't build the tower and city. However, they have never stopped communicating and exchanging in language and culture, that is the role translation has played.

— 1 —

2. History of Translation

As a means of communication, translation plays an important role in human civilization. In the West, literary translation can be traced back to 300 BC; while in China, recorded translation activities are even earlier, dating from Zhou Dynasty (1100 BC).

Both China and the West take the translation of religious scriptures as the first, such as Buddhist Scriptures (sutra) in China, Bible in the West. In China, the translation of sutra was led by 安世高，支谦，释道安，鸠摩罗什，真谛，玄奘(The last three were great translators of sutra). The second is that of science works, which are originated by 徐光启, (whose famous translations with Italian missionary 利玛窦 are《几何原理/本》《测量法义》); the third is that of literary works, such as《巴黎茶花女遗事》《黑奴吁天录》(*Uncle Tom's Cabin*),《块肉余生记》(*David Copperfield*),《王子复仇记》(*Hamlet*) by 林纾/琴南,《毁灭》《死魂灵》by 鲁迅,《海燕》《高尔基论文选集》《托尔斯泰短篇小说集》by 瞿秋白; then the translation of philosophical ones, led by 严复, whose famous translations are《天演论》《原富》《法意》.

However, not until the recent centuries, especially by the end of the 19th century did systematic study of translation get under way. And the recent decades have seen rapid development in translation theories and translation activities both at home and abroad.

3. Nature and Scope of Translation

3.1 What is translation

1) In a narrow sense

Translation means to express the meaning of a certain text of a language by using another language, e. g. English—Chinese translation/Chinese—English translation (interlingual translation 语际翻译).

2) In a broad sense

Translation can also mean those kinds of translation between a dialect and the common language of a country, between one dialect and another dialect, between the old form and the modern form of a language, like the translation between classical Chinese and modern Chinese. It also includes the transformation between signs or numbers and a language. That is, intralingual translation（语内翻译）and intersemiotic translation（符际翻译）.

3.2　Three meanings of translation

Translating: the process to translate, the activity rather than the tangible object;

A translation: the product of the process of translating, i. e. the translated text;

Translation: the abstract concept which encompasses both the process of translating and the product of that process. (Roger T. Bell, 1995)

3.3　Definitions of translation

* Translating consists in reproducing in the receptor language the closest natural equivalent of the source language message, first in terms of meaning, and second in terms of style. (Eugene A. Nida & Charles R. Taber, 1969)

* Translating is the expression in another language (or target language) of what has been expressed in another, source language, preserving semantic and stylistic equivalences. (Roger T. Bell, 1991)

* Translation is the production of a functional TT maintaining relationship with a given ST that is specified according to the intended or demanded function of the TT. (Christiane Nord, 1991)

* Translation is an acculturation process between different cultures. (André Lefevere, 1992)

* Translation is a procedure which leads from a written SLT to an optimally equivalent TLT and requires the syntactic, semantic and text-pragmatic comprehension by the translator of the original text. (Wolfram Wilss, 2001)

3.4　Is translation an art, a science or a craft/skill

Translation is first a science, which entails the knowledge and verification of the facts and the language that describe them—here, what is wrong, mistakes of truth, can be identified;

Secondly, it is a skill, which calls for appropriate language and acceptable usage;

Thirdly, an art, which distinguishes good writing from undistinguished writing and is the creative, the intuitive, sometimes the inspired, level of translation;

Lastly, a matter of taste, where argument ceases, and preference are expressed, and the variety of meritorious translation is the reflection of individual differences. (Peter Newmark, 1988)

3.5 What is a good translation

Alexander F. Tytler (1791), the 18th century British translation theorist and professor at the University of Edinburgh, described a good translation—that in which the merit of the original work is so completely transfused into another language, as to be as distinctly apprehended, and as strongly felt, by a native of the country to which that language belongs, as it is by those who speak the language of the original work.

3.6 Translator's knowledge bases and skills

Five knowledge bases: Source Language (SL) knowledge, Target Language (TL) knowledge, text-type knowledge, domain knowledge and contrastive knowledge.

Two skills: decoding (reading) + encoding (writing)

3.7 Classifications of translation

Translation covers a very broad range and has different classifications.

In terms of linguistic signs: it contains intralingual translation, interlingual translation and intersemiotic translation.

In terms of languages: there are translation from native languages into foreign languages, and that from foreign languages into native languages.

In terms of the mode: we have oral interpretation (alternating interpretation, simultaneous interpretation, sight interpretation, *etc.*), written translation, and automatic translation (machine translation).

In terms of disposal: we have full-text/complete translation, abridged/partial translation or adapted translation, and variation translation.

In terms of materials to be translated: we have translation of literary texts (novels, poems, essays, dramas, literary criticism, *etc.*), translation of practical texts (official documents, contracts and agreements, notices, regulations, ads, letters, manual books, *etc.*), translation of scientific texts (academic works/articles, experiment reports/results, manual books, *etc.*), translation of political texts (works of social sciences, research reports, speeches, *etc.*), and translation of journalistic texts (news reports, news features, news correspondences, editorials, *etc.*).

4. Principles or Criteria of Translation

4.1 Alexander Tytler (1790): three laws of translation

* It should give a complete transcript of the ideas of the original work.

* The style and manner of writing should be of the same character with that of the original.

* The translation should have all the ease of original composition.

4.2 Yan Fu (1898): triple principle of "xin, da, ya"

Faithfulness/accuracy (full and complete conveying or transmission of the original content or thought), expressiveness/smoothness (the version must be clear and flowing without any grammatical mistakes or confused sense and logic), and elegance (the use of classical Chinese before the Han Dynasty).

According to Nida (2001), the three principles of faithfulness, expressiveness and elegance should be understood not as competitive but as additive factors: faithful equivalence in meaning, expressive clarity of form, and attractive elegance that makes a text a pleasure to read.

4.3 Two commonly-accepted criteria

Faithfulness/accuracy (忠实/准确) and smoothness (通顺/流畅).

* Be faithful to the original content/meaning/views, original author's emotions and feelings, the original form and style.

* Be easy and readable in rendering, namely forceful, clear and idiomatic expression in the target language, free from stiff formula and mechanical copying from dictionaries.

5. Translation Process

Translating is a complex and fascinating task. In fact, I. A. Richard (1953) has claimed that it is probably the most complex type of event in the history of cosmos.

The process of translation consists of three phases: comprehension, expression and check. Here we just focus on the first two stages.

5.1 Comprehension

There are two famous sayings: "You know a word by the company it keeps." " No context, no text." Therefore, it is very necessary for translators to understand the word meaning through linguistic context and background knowledge.

<u>Translate the following sentences or analyze the sentence structure</u>:

(1) He saw a friend in me.

(2) She cried her eyes out.

(3) The girl soon laid the table.

(4) His fury was exaggerated.

(5) We searched him to no purpose.

(6) From life to death is man's reach.

(7) "He was really a miser." "And how!"

(8) I won't do it to save my life.

(9) Let any man come; I am his man.

(10) Theory is something but practice is everything.

(11) In learning English, grammar is not everything.

(12) "What do you think of Tom?" "Oh, he has nothing in him."

(13) I have read your articles. I expected to meet an older man.

(14) When she and he met again, each had been married to another.

(15) Dear, dear! All flesh is grass.

(16) And to think that I and these noble d'Urberwilles were one flesh all the time.

(17) But the master of the house was his mother. She was twice the man her son was, they said.

(18) The approach to the management of foreign exchange reserves by central bankers

varies across the globe, ranging from a policy of benign neglect to detailed and highly mathematical calculations of alternative moves to reduce risk and increase profitability.

世界各国央行行长们对自由兑换外汇储备的管理方法各不相同，有的国家对外汇管理采取某些宽松政策，有的国家则采取详细计算各种外汇储备的方式，以便减少风险和提高收益。

5.2 Expression

There are two main methods: literal translation and free translation.

1) Literal translation

Literal translation means "not to alter the original words and sentences", but "to keep the sentiments and style of the original". For example:

crocodile's tears 鳄鱼的眼泪   armed to the teeth 武装到牙齿

to add fuel to the fire 火上加油   to fish in troubled water 混水摸鱼

a gentlemen's agreement 君子协定   to break the record 打破纪录

2) Free translation

Free translation is used mainly to convey the meaning and spirit of the original without trying to reproduce its sentence patterns or figures of speech, i. e. "得意忘形". For example:

at sixes and sevens 乱七八糟   in two minds 三心二意

in threes and fours 三五成行   in one or two words 三言两语

one in a thousand 百里挑一   It rains cats and dogs 大雨滂沱

Translate the following sentences or choose a better version:

(1) Will a duck swim?

(2) They parted enemies.

(3) Justice has long arms.

(4) Last night I heard him driving his pigs to market.

(5) The talk about raising taxes was a red flag to many voters.

(6) She knew I knew and she knew if she got funny I'd either ruin the romance or make her marry him, so she was very friendly.

(A) 她知道我知道她和他的事，她也明白她要是跟我过不去，破坏或成全他们全在我的一念之间，所以她对我很客气。

（B）她很了解我，我很了解她；要是她遭遇困难，我得牺牲我们的浪漫，让她同他结婚，因为她待我太好了。

3）Literal translation and free translation

At the word or phrase level, we do have 100 percent literal translation or free translation, but at sentence level and beyond, it is quite common to see the combination of both literal translation and free translation.

Let's look at the following examples:

（1）Some officials often pay lip-service to education but don't work for better schools.

一些官员们经常口惠而实不至，口口声声说支持教育，却又不肯为改善学校条件做一些实际工作。

（2）During summer vacation, many college students are couch potatoes who like popping cold drinks and relaxing in front of their wide-screen high definition television sets.

暑假期间，许多大学生喜欢窝在沙发里长时间地看电视，一边手拿冰镇饮料，一边轻松地欣赏宽屏幕上的高清电视节目。

（3）The splitting of the atom was first used in warfare, but after Hiroshima and Nagasaki a grand effort began to provide electricity "too cheap to meter," freeing the world from its dependence on fossil fuels.

原子核裂变技术首先被用于战争，但是继广岛和长崎原子弹事件之后，这一伟大的发明便用来为人类提供"物美价廉"的电力，让世界摆脱对化石燃料的依赖。

6. Translation and Culture: Foreignization and Domestication

Translation and culture are inseparable. In fact, translation is a cross-lingual, cross-cultural and cross-social activity. "Domesticating translation" and "foreignizing translation" are two strategies coined by Lawrence Venuti (1995) to deal with cultural elements in translating. The former (target culture-oriented) refers to a transparent, fluent style adopted in order to minimize the strangeness of the foreign text for target language readers, while the latter (source culture-oriented) designates the type of translation "deliberately breaks target conventions by retaining something of the foreignness of the original". The key difference between them is whether we keep the foreignness or not. The most famous representatives of each school are Nida and Venuti.

Let's look at the translation of "谋事在人，成事在天". Which one is foreignization? Which one is domestication?

> Man proposes, <u>God</u> disposes. (By David Hawkes)
>
> Man proposes, <u>Heaven</u> disposes. (By Yang Xianyi)

For another example, the translation of 东风 and 西风：

> 相见时难别亦难，东风无力百花残。
>
> ——李商隐《无题》

English Version：

> It's difficult for us to meet and hard to part；
>
> The east wind is too weak to revive flowers dead.
>
> ——许渊冲译（选自《中诗英韵探胜》）

> It's a warm wind, the west wind, full of bird's cries；
>
> I never hear the west wind but tears are in my eyes.
>
> For it comes from the west lands, the old brown hill,
>
> And April's in the west wind, and daffodils.
>
> ——John Mansfield, *Ode to the West Wind*

Chinese Version：

> 这是暖风哟，西风哟，充满了小鸟的歌唱；
>
> 我每一次听到了西风，就不禁泪水哟盈眶。
>
> 因为它来自那西土，那苍老而暗黄的山峦，
>
> 西风吹来了四月，也吹来了水仙。
>
> ——余光中译

7. Translation Techniques

Translation techniques to be dealt with in the following units are: diction, addition, omission, conversion, negation, rendering of passive voice, rendering of subordinate clauses and that of long sentences.

Discussion

1. Is translation important or not? Any examples to support your idea?
2. What's your opinion on the principles or criteria of translation?
3. How do you understand literal translation and free translation?

Unit 2 Comparisons between Chinese and English Language

1. Language Features

1.1 Analytic and synthetic language

Chinese is an analytic language with less inflections: no fixed part of speech, no inflections in different tenses, voices, moods of a verb. And phrases and sentences are formed according to word order and empty words, such as 学习政治, 政治学习; 克服困难,困难问题. Here the parts of speech of 学习, 政治, 困难 are determined by their word order, context and logic. However, English is both analytic and synthetic language with rich inflections: inflections in persona, tense, voice, mood, tone and non-predicate form (infinitive, participle) for a verb; single or plural form for a noun; comparative form for an adjective or an adverb. Phrases and sentences are formed according to word order and auxiliaries. Therefore, when rendering into Chinese, we need change the parts of speech or add words to express different inflections in English. For example:

(1) His being neglected by the host added his uneasiness.

主人的冷遇使他更加不舒服。

(2) Oxford has, or had till yesterday, fewer students than the University of Toronto.

无论现在还是过去，牛津的在校学生数都比多伦多大学少得多。

(3) They told me that Professor Liu would have been teaching here for twenty years by this winter.

他们告诉我说，到今年冬天刘教授在这里教书就要满二十年了。

1.2 Static and dynamic description

Static description is more used in English, while dynamic description in Chinese. As a result, English sentences overuse nouns, prepositions, adjectives and adverbs; while verbs, 4-character phrases and short sentences dominate Chinese. Therefore, it is quite natural to make some conversions in parts of speech and sentence structures in translation. For example:

（1）It is because he is modest and thoughtful that he is respected by his colleagues.

正是由于他为人谦虚、体贴别人，他才赢得同事的尊重。

（2）The computer is a far more careful and industrious inspector than human beings.

计算机比人检查得更仔细、更勤快。

（3）It is rather for us to be here dedicated to the great task remaining before us——that government of the people, by the people, for the people, shall not perish from the earth.

倒是我们应该在这里把自己奉献给仍然留在我们面前的伟大任务，以便使这个民有、民治、民享的政府永世长存。

（4）进入学要考试，择优录取。

Admission to university is by examination and selection.

（5）烟尘滚滚，人声嘈杂，夜色愈深，一切都陷入混乱之中。

The dust, the uproar and the growing dark threw everything into chaos.

（6）社会主义的主要目标是解放和发展生产力，消灭剥削，消除贫富两极分化，最终达到共同富裕。

The main goals of socialism are the liberation and development of productive forces, the elimination of exploitation and polarization between the rich and the poor and the final achievement of common prosperity.

2. Words

In comparison with Chinese, English words are more flexible both in form and in meaning.

Put the following sentences into Chinese or English, paying attention to the word "heavy" and Chinese character "意见":

(1) He is a media heavy.

(2) His father is a heavy drinker.

(3) This car is very heavy on oil.

(4) This dessert is not bad, but a little heavy.

(5) He is so heavy that he needs extra-large shirts.

(6) After work, she went home with a heavy heart.

(7) The rain is falling heavier tonight than last night.

(8) There was a heavy fragrance of flowers and lemon trees.

(9) This is a heavy news to everyone that there will be a war in the next decade.

(10) 两个好朋友因为钱的问题在闹意见。

(11) 人们对明星代言药品广告持不同意见。

(12) 近年来，人们对北京的雾霾很有意见。

(13) 换专业之前应该征求家长和老师的意见。

(14) 对气候变化这个话题，我想补充几点意见。

2.1 Correspondence at the word level

1) Full correspondence

This is most evidently shown in the translation of proper nouns and technical terms. For example：

Marxism = 马克思主义　　　　　penicillin = 盘尼西林(青霉素)

基因 = gene　　　　　　　　　白血病 = leukemia

2) Half correspondence

It refers to multiple equivalents of the same or different meanings of the given word. For example：

wife：妻子、爱人、夫人、太太、老婆、老伴、媳妇、堂客、内人……

president：总统、总裁、主席、董事长、议长、委员长、会长、社长、校长……

cousin：堂兄、堂弟、堂姐、堂妹、表哥、表弟、表姐、表妹、亲戚、亲属……

carry：搬、运、送、提、拎、挑、担、抬、背、扛、搂、抱、端、举、夹、捧……

车辆：vehicle, car, carriage, bicycle, tricycle, motor, truck, automobile…

医生：doctor, physician, surgeon, medical man, pediatrician, psychiatrist…

说: speak, talk, tell, relate, argue, swear, shout, cry, retort, demand, query, protest...

羊: sheep, goat, ram, ewe, lamb...

3) Zero correspondence

Due to unique culture of English and Chinese, we can't always find equivalents of some words, culture-loaded words in particular, in this case an explanation or transliteration is needed. For example:

Teenager: 13~19 岁的少年

阳: *Yang* (strong active male principle or force in the world)

2.2 Word order

Every nation has its own unique ways to generate some idiomatic expressions, and so are English and Chinese with different sequences in word formation. For example:

track and field 田径   sooner or later 迟早   one and the same 同一的

one and only 唯一的   rain or shine 不论晴雨   heart-warming 暖人心的

tough-minded 意志坚定的   East China 华东

share the weal and woe 祸福与共

back and forth, to and fro 前前后后,来来去去

suffer from cold and hunger 饥寒交迫

inconsistency of deeds with words 言行不一

food, clothing, shelter/housing and transportation 衣食住行

3. Sentence Elements

3.1 Subject

In English sentences, noun, noun phrase, pronoun, number, nouns for time and place, gerund, infinitive, substantive clause, "it" and "there be" pattern can serve as the subject, while the subject in Chinese sentences can be noun, noun phrase, pronoun, number, nouns for time and place, verb, verb phrase, adjective, sentence and "的" phrase. For example:

1. 房子盖在西院。

2. 我们盖了一栋房子。

3. 西院盖了一栋房子。

4. 去年又盖了一栋房子。

5. 台上坐着主席团。

6. 这是哪儿?

7. 今儿不开会。

8. 跑跑跳跳助消化。

9. 吃饭得使筷子。

10. 15 是个奇数。

11. 财源有限,开销无穷。

12. 倾囊相助是一种美德。

13. 他的事你不必着急。

14. 聪明并不意味着成功。

15. 冷静才能计算正确。

16. 学得最好的有奖。

17. 走一步看一步。

18. 街上有很多人。

19. 沿路都是小商店。

20. 种瓜得瓜,种豆得豆。

21. 一个人干就可以了。

22. 他信了你的话才怪呢。

23. 猫比狗凶是会有的。

24. 窗外传来了一阵笑声。

25. 学会数理化,走遍天下都不怕。

26. 慢,不碍事;太快,容易出错。

27. 庖有肥肉,厩有肥马,民有饥色,野有饿莩。

28. 打是疼,骂是爱,不打不骂千奇百怪。

Special features: there are sometimes sentences with double subjects or omitted subject in Chinese; when rendering into English, we need to choose one subject or supply a new one. For example:

29. 这个人脾气倔。

30. 活到老,学到老。

31. 又盖了许多高楼。

32. 不许在此交谈。

33. 他一边吃,一边瞪着大眼睛环顾四周,不禁暗自发笑:眼前这一派富丽奢华,说不定某一天会统统落进我的手掌心。

He could not help, too, rolling his large eyes round him as he ate, and chuckling with the possibility that he might one day be lord of all this scene of almost unimaginable luxury and splendour.

3.2 Predicate

In English sentences, only verb (transitive verb, intransitive verb, link verb, auxiliary verb) can serve as the predicate, while the predicate in Chinese sentences can be verb, verb phrase, noun, noun phrase, adjective, adjective phrase, quantifier, prepositional phrase, sentence and "的" phrase. For example:

1. 我知道这事。

2. 谁说/干的?

3. 我热死了。   4. 这瓜可甜了。

5. 这鞋又小又旧。   6. 这个人是好人。

7. 这姑娘眼睛大。   8. 每人一本。

9. 这男孩 16 岁了。   10. 他一身臭汗。

11. 他性子急躁。   12. 这个菜浪咸。

13. 这孩子记性好。   14. 中国地大物博。

15. 你把我吓坏了。   16. 你这个人小题大做。

17. 8 月 15 家家吃月饼。   18. 不下雨已经 2 个月了。

19. 这种行为浪不道德。   20. 党的恩情比山高，比海深。

21. 我不是不懂，是不想说。   22. 这个问题工会要解决。

23. 朋友旧的好，衣服新的好。   24. 家事、国事、天下事，事事关心。

25. 墙上芦苇头重脚轻根底浅，山中竹笋嘴尖皮厚腹中空。

Special features: it is quite common that there is more than one verb or one subject/predicate in a Chinese sentence, while only one subject and one predicate verb in an English sentence. Therefore, when translating Chinese into English, it is necessary to choose one subject, and one verb as the predicate verb, others as the non-predicate forms (gerund or infinitive). For example:

26. 他经常请客赴宴。   27. 我记得他去过华盛顿。

28. 李教授总是站着讲课。   29. 我有个朋友住在温哥华。

30. 孩子们跑着来迎接我们。   31. 他经常带学生到工厂去参观。

32. 让我们打开窗户换换新鲜空气。   33. 他拿了一本字典，开始准备功课。

34. 他想打电话与她约个时间见面叙谈。   35. 下周四他准备请假坐飞机回家探亲。

3.3 Attributive

1) Words as an attributive

In a Chinese sentence, attributive words usually precede the words being modified, and it is also true for most English words. But there are some exceptions: When an adjective modifies "something, anything, nothing, everything; someone/somebody, anyone/anybody, none/nobody, everyone/everybody"; the word ends with "-able/ible", and when used in the sentence having "all, every, only", the attributive must follow the word being modified. For example:

He is the only person reliable.

I have something important to tell you.

We must try to help them every way possible.

We should try every means possible to deal with the environmental problems.

Note：when more than one adjective modify the noun in a Chinese or an English sentence, it usually follows a principle of either subjective→objective sequence or *vice versa*. For example：

a small round wooden table：一张木头小圆桌

advanced foreign experience：外国的先进经验

世界先进水平：advanced world level

近代先进科学技术：advanced modern science and technology

全国性大规模的油气勘探：large-scale national oil and gas exploration

2）Phrases or clauses as an attributive

English attributive phrases and clauses usually follow the words being modified（the antecedent）, whereas in Chinese, such phrases and clauses always precede the words being modified. For example：

（1）It was a bolt **from the blue**.

这真是个晴天霹雳。

（2）The woman **holding a baby in her arms** is waiting to see the doctor.

那个手里抱着婴儿的妇女正等着医生看病。

（3）A rocket is like a tube of fuel **closed at one end and open at the other**.

火箭就像一个一端封闭一端开口的燃料管。

（4）Most of the information **that we have got from the Internet** is accurate and authentic.

我们从因特网上得到的大部分信息都准确、可信。

3.4 Adverbial

1）Adverb serving as the adverbial put before adjective or conjunction

In this case, we can keep the original order or add "得" after verbs when rendering English into Chinese. For example：

（1）China is especially rich in natural resources.

中国的自然资源特别丰富。

（2）I can't speak English so fluently as she does.

我英语说得没有她这么流利。

（3）This new computer moves amazingly fast.

这台新电脑运行的速度快得惊人。

Exception：The word "enough" is put after the adjective or adverb.

（4）The room is large enough to seat all of us.

这房间够大，我们全部坐得下。

（5）He didn't work hard enough then.

那时，他工作不够努力。

2）Adverbial of time，place and manner

Both adverbials of time and place are often placed at the end of a sentence in English, while Chinese sentences often have them at the beginning. If these two kinds of adverbials coexist in a single sentence, the adverbial of time usually follows those of place in English, but they are just in the reverse order in Chinese. If there are adverbials of time, place and manner in an English sentence, the order should be subject ＋ predicate ＋ object ＋ manner ＋ place ＋ time, while subject ＋ time ＋ place ＋ manner ＋predicate ＋ object in a Chinese sentence. For example：

His grandmother passed away in hospital at 2. 30 a. m. on July 15, 2007.

他祖母于 2007 年 7 月 15 日凌晨 2 点 30 分在医院逝世。

Many college students read English aloud in the open every morning.

很多大学生每天早晨在室外高声朗读英语。

3）Adverbial phrases

Adverbial phrases of "condition", "purpose", "concession" or "cause or reason", and so on in English may stand either before or after a principal clause; however, when translated into Chinese, they are normally placed before the principal clause.

（1）He failed at last with all his efforts. （or：With all his efforts he fails at last. ）

不管他怎样努力，最后还是没有成功。

（2）We need to do much visual work to effectively present a website to clients.

为了向客户有效地展示一个网站，我们需要做很多视觉上的工作。

4. Sentence Structure

4.1 SV *vs*. TR

English sentences are of typical Subject + Verb (SV) structure, while theme/topic + rheme/remark (TR) structure in Chinese ones. This can be seen from the sentences given in subject part mentioned above.

4.2 Loose *vs*. periodic sentence

An English sentence is just like a bunch of grapes with short stem (subject, verb or object) and lots of fruits (attributives and adverbials). That is to say, most of English sentences have loose structure, so they are called loose sentences with the most important part at the beginning and the least important in the end. While a Chinese sentence, either like a bamboo or a dish of pearl, has a periodic structure with the most important in the end. Therefore, it is quite common to see the conversion between loose and periodic structure in English and Chinese translation. For example:

(1) It may seem strange that in this modern electronic time, the physicists are still a very long way from understanding the ultimate structure of matter or existence.

当今电子时代，物理学家们还远没有弄清物质/存在的最终结构，这似乎有些不可思议。

(2) I am always amazed when I hear people saying that sport creates goodwill between the nations, and that if only the common peoples of the world could meet one another at football or cricket, they would have no inclination to meet on the battlefield.

每当我听人们说体育运动可建立国家之间的友谊，还说各国民众若在足球场或板球场上交锋，就不愿在战场上残杀的时候，我总是惊愕不已。

(3) 如蒙早日寄来样品或产品册，不胜感激。

It would be appreciated if samples or brochures could be soon forwarded.

(4) 为了确保自己的知识和专业技能不过时，如今的工程师必须毕生不断学习。

Today's engineers must study throughout their careers to make sure that their knowledge and expertise do not become obsolete.

4.3 Parataxis *vs.* hypotaxis

As some linguists suggest, English is more hypotactic（形合）, where syntactical relations are expressed by connectives, while Chinese is more paratactic（意合）, in which clauses or phrases are placed one after another without coordinating connectives. Therefore, it is necessary for translators to convert from paratactic structure to hypotactic one or *vice versa*. For example：

（1）We'd better go back, **since** the wind is too strong **and** we can't set sail.

风太大，船不能开，回去吧。

（2）**Once** the principal contradiction is grasped, all problems can be readily solved.

抓住了主要矛盾，一切问题就可以迎刃而解。

（3）我买了 4 本书，（这 4 本书）一共（花了我）17 元，（我把它们）拿回家一看，（我发现这些书）都是半新半旧的。

I bought 4 books **which** cost **me** 17 yuan. **When I** took **them** back home, **I** found **they** were just second hand.

（4）（若）知己（又）知波，（则）（虽）百战（而）不殆；（若）不知波而知己，（则）（将）一胜（及）一负；（若）不知波（又）不知己，（则）每战（将）必殆。

You can fight a hundred battles without defeat **if you** know the enemy **as well as** yourself. **You** will win one battle **and** lose one battle **if you** know yourself **but** are in the dark about the enemy. **You** will lose every battle **if you** are in the dark about **both** the enemy **and** yourself.

4.4 Passive voice *vs.* active voice

Passive voice is widely used in English, especially in scientific literatures, but less commonly used in Chinese. The rendering of passive voices will be dealt with in Unit 8. Here let's look at an example to see how often the passive and active voices are used in English and Chinese.

Vegetable oil has been known from antiquity. No household can get on without it, for it is used in cooking. Perfumes may be made from the oils of certain flowers. Soaps are made from vegetable and animal oils.

植物油自古以来就为人们所熟悉。任何家庭都离不开它，因为做饭的时候就要用它。有些花儿产生的油可以用来制造香水。植物油和动物油还可以用来制作肥皂。

For the above sentence, four passive voices are converted into three active voices and one passive voice in Chinese sentence.

4.5 Inverted sentence *vs.* natural order

* Interrogative inversion

How did you solve the problem?

这个问题你是怎么解决的?

* Imperative inversion

"Speak you," said Mr. Black, "Speak you, good fellow!"

布莱克先生命令道:"说,说吧! 伙计!"

* Exclamatory inversion

How beautiful is this place!

这地方好漂亮啊!

* Hypothetical inversion

Had you come yesterday, you could have seen her here.

要是你昨天来了,你就会在这里看到她。

* Balance inversion

Through a gap came an elaborately described ray.

从一个空隙透出一束精心描绘的光线。/一束精心描绘的光线从一个空隙透出。

* Link inversion

On this depends the whole argument.

整个争论都以此为论据。

* Signpost inversion

By strategy it meant something wider.

战略的意义比较广。

* Negative inversion

Never has the company had any experience in exploring the shale gas in deep sea.

该公司在开采深海页岩气方面从来就没有什么经验。

5. Sentence Order

5.1 Principle of temporal sequence

English sentences are generally bound by syntax and grammar, and the sentence order is flexible, while a Chinese sentence usually follows the sequential order of an event (from the past to the present). For example:

阅读(先阅后读):reading

汗流浃背:soaked with sweat

跑了和尚,跑不了庙。The monk can run away, but the temple can't run with him.

Nothing has happened since we parted. 我们分开后,什么事情都没有发生。

Rocket research has confirmed a strange fact which had already been suspected: there is a "high-temperature belt" in the atmosphere, with its center roughly thirty miles above the ground.

人们早就怀疑大气层中有一个高温带,其中心在距地面约 30 英里高的地方。利用火箭加以研究以后,这一奇异的事实已得到了证实。

5.2 Principle of spatial sequence

Spatial sequence in English is from the small to the big, while just opposite in Chinese. For example:

2015 年晚秋九月的某一天:On someday in September of the late autumn in 2015

北京市海淀区学院路丁 11 号:D11 Xueyuan Road, Haidian District, Beijing

5.3 Logical order

Adverbial of cause, result, condition, supposition and purpose in English can be preceded or followed the main clause, while in Chinese it usually follows the order: cause→result, condition→result, introduction→transition, action→purpose. For example:

松散 loose   油光光 brilliantly polished

泣不成声 choke with sobs   积劳成疾 fall ill through constant overwork

The plan for a new office building went ahead regardless of local opposition.

尽管当地人反对,建设新办公楼的计划照常进行。

I am a poor man, but I have this consolation: I am poor by accident, not by design.

我贫穷,但以此自慰:我穷得偶然,而非天命。

Translation Practice

Ⅰ. Put the following paragraphs into Chinese/English.

1. For many people, the need for human translators seems paradoxical in this age of computers since modern computer can be loaded with dictionaries and grammars, why not let computers do the work? Computers can perform certain simple interlingual tasks, providing there is sufficient pre-editing and post-editing. But neither advertising brochure nor lyric poetry can ever be reduced to the kind of logic required of computer programs. Computer printouts of translations can often be understood, if the persons involved already know what the text is supposed to say. But the results of machine translating are usually in an unnatural form of language and sometimes just plain weird. Furthermore, real improvements will not come from merely doctoring the program or adding rules. The human brain is not only digital and analogical, it also has a built-in system of values which gives it a componentially incalculable advantage over machines. Human translation will always be necessary for any text which is stylistically appealing and semantically complex — which includes most of what is worthy of communicating in another language. (Eugene A. Nida, 1993)

2. 翻译的意义是将词句从一种语言转换成另一种语言。简单地讲,它是用与原作不同的语言将作者的真正意思准确地复述出来的一种艺术。从以上翻译的定义来看,我们知道词句的原意必须尽可能保持准确,不可有所增删。翻译者的任务只是变换词汇而不是改变其意思。因此,翻译有两种要素:准确性与表达性。

准确性是翻译的首要条件。译者必须谨慎地遵循原作者的意思。字词的选择与句式结构必须如实传达原作的思想。表达性是使译文易于理解。换言之,译者必须用自己的文字尽可能地将原作思想清楚而有力地表达出来。准确性是使译文的意义确切无误,而表达性则是使译文生动、引人入胜。

Ⅱ. Choose a better translation.

1. It occurred to him that one cigarette would comfort him.

（A）这时,他想到,一支香烟也许能给他带来点安慰。

（B）这时，他想到，吸支香烟也许能解解愁。

（C）这时，他想到，一支香烟也许能安慰他一下。

（D）他突然想起，一支香烟也许能帮他消愁。

2. From here we can see the whole grassland which is very beautiful, and the sight of it filled us with longing.

（A）从那里我们可以看见整个草原，非常美丽，见到后使我们心里充满了渴望。

（B）从这里望过去，整个草原一览无遗，美不胜收，真叫我们心驰神往。

（C）遥望草原，一览无遗，美不胜收，令人心驰神往。

（D）从这里我们可以看见整个草原，它是那么美丽，令人向往。

Unit 3　Translation Techniques（1）Diction

By "diction" we mean proper choice of words and phrases in translation on the basis of accurate comprehension of the original.

In translation practices, what perplexes a translator most is how to find the equivalents in the target language to be translated into, as word meanings vary with the change of collocation or context.

As regards this phenomenon, there are two sayings: "The meaning of a word is its use in the language." "Each word, when used in a new context, is a new word."

1. Methods to Discriminate the Original Meaning of an English Word

1.1 Judging from the word formation

English vocabulary consists of a large number of compound words, many of which come from derivation, affixation, blending, acronym, or clipping. So a good command of English word formation will help us discriminate their meanings well.

A typical example is word "pneumonoultramicroscopicsilicovolcanoconiosis"（硅酸盐沉着病,矽肺病）, which consists of the following parts: pneumono-(of lung) + ultra-(beyond) + micro (very small) + scopic-(of viewing or observing) + silico-(of silicon) + volcano + coni-(koni, of dust) + osis (forming the name of a disease).

1.2 Judging from different branches of learning and specialties

Examples of the word "base":

（1）He is on the second base.

他在二垒。（体育）

（2）The lathe should be set on a firm base.

车床应安装在坚实的底座上。（机械）

（3）Line AB is the base of the triangle ABC.

AB 线是三角形 ABC 的底边。（数学）

（4）As we all know, a base reacts with an acid to form a salt.

众所周知，碱与酸反应生成盐。（化学）

（5）A transistor has three electrodes：the emitter, the base and the collector.

晶体管有三个电极，即发射极、基极和集电极。（电子）

1.3 Judging from different contexts

Take the word "work" for example：

（1）It is a work of art.

（2）They often work in the factories.

（3）Yesterday we did a good day's work.

（4）He knows how to work this machine.

（5）We have read through the works by Einstein.

（6）There was no automobile works in Hefei in the 1950s.

（7）Some satellite relay stations do a different kind of work.

（8）The works of these watches are all home-produced and wear well.

（9）The amount of work is equal to the product of the force by the distance.

（10）Sustainable management of resources remains to be seen whether it will work.

1.4 Judging from different collocations

Look at the word "make" with different collocations：

（1）Molecules are made up of atoms.

（2）Hydrogen and oxygen make water.

（3）Female spiders make webs in trees and flowers.

（4）The very abstractness of mathematics makes it useful.

（5）With electricity, radio communication is made possible.

（6）Most substances make an increase in volume when they are heated.

（7）Great advances have been made in China's science and technology.

（8）We will make use of a number of new sources of energy in the future.

（9）We are determined to make greater contributions to our environmental protection.

（10）They are trying to make a new type of electric motor to meet the needs of production.

2. Techniques of Translating a Given English Word

2.1 Transplant

Transplant means translating without alteration, namely literal translation of the corresponding parts of an English word.

dataphone 数据送话（机）　　　　microwave 微波

particulate matter 颗粒物　　　　splashdown 溅落

ironmaking 炼铁（业）　　　　copytron = copy + electron 电子复写（技术）

2.2 Pictographic translation/morphotranslation

English letters are often used to name the objects which are similar to the letter in shape. This kind of terminology is generally morphotranslated, which is applied in the following three cases：

1）Choose the characters that can denote the shape of the original object and/or English letter

T-square 丁字尺　　　　T-track 锤形泾迹　　　　I-column 工字柱

H-beam 工字梁　　　　U-bend 马蹄弯头　　　　U-steel 槽钢

V-belt 三角皮带　　　　V-slot 三角形槽　　　　Z-iron Z字铁

Y-curve 叉形曲线　　　　X-brace 交叉支撑　　　　O-ring 环形圈

2）Keep the letter not translated, but add a character "形" to it

A—bedplate　A 形底座　　　　D—valve　D 形阀

C—network　C 形网络　　　　M—wing　M 形机翼

3) Keep the letter not translated, use the letter to stand for a concept

N-region　　N 区(电子剩余区，即电子导电区)

AT-cut　　　AT 切片(切割方向与光轴成 35°角的晶片)

L-electron　　L 层电子(原子核外第二层的电子)

X-ray　　　X 射线(波长为 $10^{-10} \sim 10^{-6}$ 厘米的电磁波)

2.3 Transliteration

This technique is most frequently used in dealing with proper nouns (especially the names of people and places, trademarks, culture-loaded words, *etc.*). Besides, it is also used in cases of coinage where no existing Chinese expression is available.

Wall Street 华尔街　　　　　　Easy Joy 易捷(便利店)

clone 克隆　　　　　　　　　nylon 尼龙

Fonterra 恒天然(新西兰乳业巨头)　Pentium 奔腾(计算机激处理器)

quark 夸克(理论上设想的三种不带正整电荷的更基本的粒子通称)

2.4 Transliteration and free translation

kilowatt 千瓦　　　　　　　　decibel 分贝

Translation Practice

I. Put the following sentences into Chinese, paying attention to the bold words.

1. Nothing is the **matter** with the microscope.

2. May I advance my opinion on the **matter**?

3. It's no **matter** whether you give me the data early or late.

4. Waterpower has become a **matter** of great economic importance.

5. He got at the essence of **matter** by breaking through phenomenalism.

6. The **matter** in the scientific writing is good but the style is deplorable.

7. All the phenomena of nature are shown to us in time and in space through **matter**.

8. Actually the more the physicists discover, the more utterly amazing the **matter** of existence will be.

9. Men of science in their experiments claimed to have discovered what they believe to be the ultimate structure of **matter**, the quarks.

10. The fourth **power** of two is sixteen.

11. By **power** is meant the rate of doing work.

12. Electric **power** can be transmitted over a long distance.

13. The output **power** of a machine is always smaller than its input **power**.

14. The higher the speed of the space vehicle, the greater its **power** consumption.

15. Large quantities of steam are used by modern industry in the generation of **power**.

16. The surfaces of ceramics must be checked by examining them under a 20 **power** binocular microscope.

17. Accompanying the strong wish for overall reduction in weight and volume is the need to reduce the **power** consumption of components and equipments.

18. The combining **power** of one element in the compound must equal the combing **power** of the other element.

19. The Declaration consists of three parts: firstly, a profound and eloquent **statement** of political philosophy — the philosophy of democracy and of freedom; secondly, a **statement** of specific grievances designed to prove that George III had subverted American freedom; thirdly, a solemn **statement** of independence and pledge of support for that policy.

20. I **got** on horseback within ten minutes after I **got** your letter. When I **got** to Canterbury, I **got** a chaise for town, but I **got** wet through, and have **got** such a cold that I shall not **get** rid of it in a hurry. I **got** to the Treasury about noon, but first of all **got** shaved and dressed. I soon **got** into the secret of **getting** a memorial before the Board, but I could not **get** an answer then; however I **got** intelligence from a messenger that I should **get** one next morning. As soon as I **got** back to my inn, I **got** my supper and then **got** to bed. When I **got** up next morning, I **go** my breakfast, and having **got** dressed, I **got** out in time to **get** an answer to my memorial. As soon as I **got** it, I **got** into a chaise, and **got** back to Canterbury by three, and **got** nothing for you, and so adieu. (E. C. Brewer's *Dictionary of Phrase and Fable*)

II. Put the following sentences into English, paying attention to the word "红".

1. 晚会开得红红火火。

2. 她曾经是老板的红人。

3. 听说他俩从来未红过脸。

4. 他们的日子越过越红火。

5. 他通宵没睡，眼睛都熬红了。

6. 他年纪轻轻却已看破了红尘。

7. 喝了几杯酒，他脸上红扑扑的。

8. 一见别人收入比他多，他就眼红。

9. 三十年代他红得发紫，战后就默默无闻了。

10. 今年我们厂是满堂红，各项指标都提前完成了。

11. 他的脸被火红的太阳晒得黑黑的，一副健康的样子。

Unit 4   Translation Techniques(2)
Amplification

1. Amplification

Amplification, also called addition, means supplying necessary words in the translation on the basis of accurate comprehension of the original.

1.1 Adding words to make an abstract concept clear

correctness 正确性   redundancy 多余信息

solution 解决方法   jealousy 嫉妒心理

best-sellerdom 畅销圈子   evolution 进化过程

innovation 革新措施   derivation 推导过程

backwardness 落后状态   preparation 准备工作

(1) His uneasy **cheerfulness** was painful to watch.

他那高兴而不安的**神情**，叫人看起来就感到痛心。

(2) What the people in the Middle East Area wanted most was an end of **uncertainties**.

中东地区的人们最渴望的就是结束这摇摆不定的**局面**。

(3) When the **exploration** was completed, the two astronauts on the moon would join the moon ship once more.

完成勘察**工作**之后，登上月球的两个宇航员便重新回到船舱内。

(4) There is more to their life than political and social and economic problems; more than transient **everydayness**.

他们的生活远不止那些政治的、社会的和经济的问题，远不止一时的**柴米油盐问题**。

1.2 Adding words to make a concrete concept abstract

（1）War in Lebanon has become an **institution**.

在黎巴嫩，打仗交火已经成了司空见惯的事。

（2）He is a bright student **floundering** because of poor study habits.

他是一个聪明的学生，但因学习习惯不良而学得很吃力。

（3）Electric power became the **servant** of man only after the motor was invented.

电动机发明之后，电才开始造福于人类。

1.3 Adding words indicating plural nouns

We know that there is no change of forms for Chinese plural nouns, while English nouns have but with few quantity words. So, in English-Chinese translation, we have to add words like overlapping words, numerals, words of generalization, *etc.* to express the concept of plural.

（1）You must know the **properties** of the instrument before you use it.

在使用仪器前，必须弄清它的各种性能。

（2）Note that the **words** "velocity" and "speed" require explanation.

请注意，"速度"和"速率"这两个词需要解释。

（3）The chess board is the world: the **pieces** are the phenomena of the universe.

棋盘宛如世界：一个个棋子仿佛世间的种种现象。

（4）Professional **schools** began to be founded as the demand for engineers steadily increased in the 1950s.

20 世纪 50 年代由于对工程师的需求不断增加，人们开始建立一批批的职业学校。

1.4 Adding omitted words conveying original meaning

（1）Studies serve for delight, for ornament, and for ability.

读书足以怡情，足以傅采，足以长才。

（2）Ice is the solid state, water the liquid state, and water vapor the gaseous state.

冰是固态，水是液态，水蒸气是气态。

（3）Reading exercises one's eyes; speaking, one's tongue; while writing, one's mind.

阅读训练人的眼睛，说话**训练**人的口齿，写作**训练**人的思维。

1.5 Adding necessary connectives

（1）Liquids contract in freezing; water is an exception.

液体冻结时收缩，**但**水却例外。

（2）His reputation and achievements outlive him.

虽然他已经去世，**可是**他的名声和成就依然存在。

（3）The best lubricant cannot maintain oil films between the surfaces of engineering gears.

即使是最好的润滑油，在齿合处也不能保住油膜。

1.6 Adding necessary verbs for collocation and smoothness

（1）There is a struggle for existence among all plants and animals.

所有动植物之间都**存在**着生存竞争。

（2）The world needn't be afraid of a possible shortage of coal, oil, natural gas or other sources of fuel for the future.

世界无需担心可能**出现**煤、石油、天然气或其他燃料来源短缺的问题。

（3）Before the euro, European nations prospered better than anyone dreamed by rebuilding their national markets.

在采用欧元之前，欧元区各国重建了国内市场，**实现**了超越任何人想象的繁荣。

1.7 Adding explanatory words making implied meaning clear

（1）A word and stone let go cannot be recalled.

说出的话，**就像扔**出的石头，是收不回来的。

（2）Anna was thin and black, a very umbrella of woman.

安娜是一个又黑又瘦的女人，**上身粗大，下身细长**，简直像一把雨伞。

（3）American President Eisenhower was not so bold as General Eisenhower.

艾森豪威尔当**总统的时候**可没有他当**将军的时候**果敢。

1.8 Adding words to express different tenses

Auxiliary verbs（will, be, have）are used in English to express different tenses, but in Chinese we have to resort to some words , such as"曾、曾经、已(经)、过、了"(for perfect tense);"正(在)、在、着……"(for progressive tense);"将、要、会、就、便、了"(for future tense);"过去、以前、曾(经)、当时"(for past tense);"现在、目前"(for present tense); and "一直、一向"(for continuous perfect tense).

(1) I was, and remain, grateful for the part he played in my success.

我的成功都应归功于他，对此我**过去**很感激，**现在**仍很感激。

(2) They had always been able to control things. Now control was getting away from all of them.

他们**从前一向**是能够控制局面的，现在他们都**正在**失去控制能力。

1.9 Adding classifiers

In English, there is only "a/an/the" or "a piece of", *etc.* to modify the single noun, while in Chinese, different nouns require the use of different classifiers, such as"一堆，一只，一个，一件，一张，一颗，一块，一副，一根，一辆，一轮，一位，一台，一扇，一本，一行，一种，一方，一项". And even some classifiers can be used to express a certain action, for example，"停一下，休息一下，吵了一顿"，*etc.*

(1) He gave her a gentle push.

他轻轻地推了她**一下**。

(2) He made a speech, eloquently advocating his company of the future.

他发表了**一篇**大论，振振有词地把他未来的公司鼓吹**一番**。

1.10 Adding auxiliary words indicating different tones and moods

(1) Don't take it seriously. I'm just making fun of you.

不要认真**嘛**！我不过开玩笑**罢了**。

(2) As for me, I didn't agree with him from the very beginning.

我**呢**，从一开始就不赞成他的观点。

2. Repetition

Repetition is also a kind of amplification. It is to repeat any word(s) or component of the original. Repetition can be used in the following cases：

2.1 Repeating the repeated part

（1）They **tried** and **tried** and at last succeeded in starting the car.

他们**试**了又**试**，最后终于成功发动了汽车。

（2）**In some areas** American firms are still ahead, **in some areas** they are **average**, and **in some areas** they are behind, but on average they are **average**.

在某些领域美国公司依然领先，**在某些领域**他们处于**中等水平**，而有些领域他们已经落后，但平均来说他们处于**中等水平**。

2.2 Repeating the omitted part with the same Chinese words

（1）The central authorities want to develop industry, and so do the local authorities.

中央要发展工业，地方也要**发展工业**。

（2）Reading makes a full man; conference a ready man; and writing an exact man.

读书使人充实，讨论**使人**机智，笔记**使人**准确。

（3）Confidence is power; the power to attract, to persuade, to influence, and to succeed.

信心是力量，是一种吸引**力**、说服**力**、影响**力**和取得成功的**动力**。

2.3 Repeating the omitted part with different Chinese words

（1）Everyone enjoys applause, compliment and praise.

人人都愿意**博得**掌声，**听到**赞扬，或**受到**称颂。

（2）A scientist constantly tried to defeat his hypotheses, his theories and his conclusions.

科学家经常要**否定**自己的假设，**推翻**自己的理论，**放弃**自己的结论。

2.4 Repeating for making the sense clear

（1）Whoever works hard will be respected.

谁努力工作，**谁**就会受到尊敬。

（2）Finally she became a successful entrepreneur—all by herself.

最终她成为一个成功的企业家——一个白手起家的**企业家**。

3. Amplification and Repetition in Chinese-English Translation

They are mainly used in the following cases.

3.1 Adding necessary connectives

（1）虚心使人进步，骄傲使人落后。

Modesty helps one to go forward, **whereas** conceit makes one lag behind.

（2）那工作搞不出名堂，他没干。

He did not take the job **because** it was a blind alley.

（3）汽油贵得惊人，我们就很少用车。

Because of fantastically high price of gasoline, we seldom used our car.

3.2 Adding necessary pronouns

（1）这本畅销书对读者产生了巨大的影响。

The bestseller had a great impact on **its** readers.

（2）必须勤学苦练，才能精通一门外国语。

One must study hard before mastering a foreign language.

（3）交出译文之前，必须读几遍，看看有没有要修改的地方。

Before handing in **your** translation, **you** have to read **it** over and over again and see if there is anything in **it** to be corrected or improved.

3.3 Adding necessary background information to make the English version clear

（1）三个臭皮匠，赛过诸葛亮。

Three cobblers with their wits combined exceed Zhuge Liang's **master mind**. / Two heads are better than one.

（2）他这分明是班门弄斧。

He is just showing off his proficiency with the axe before Lu Ban (**the master carpenter**) / To teach a fish to swim.

3.4 Repeating the original repeated words with same or different words

（1）没有调查就**没有**发言权。

He who makes **no** investigation and study has **no** right to speak.

（2）他的一贯作风就是该**工作**时就**工作**，该**玩**时就**玩**。

What he always persists in is to **work** while he **works**, and to **play** while he **plays**.

（3）在二进制里，2 用 010 表示，3 用 011 表示，4 用 100 表示。

In the binary scale, 2 is **expressed** as 010; 3 is **given** as 011; 4 is **represented** as 100.

Translation Practice

Ⅰ. Translate the following sentences, using the technique of amplification.

1. Metallurgy treats of the deriving of metals and their properties.

2. Without moving parts, maintenance requirements are cut to a minimum.

3. They were then friendly to me and my opinions considering my health.

4. There were rows of buildings which the old lady had never seen before.

5. Decisiveness, perseverance and flexibility are keys for people to succeed in business.

6. His work made it impossible for him to get home oftener than every other weekend.

7. Were there no electric pressure in a conductor, the electron flow would not take place in it.

8. The operation of electric generators is based on this relationship between magnetism and electricity.

9. The major problem in fabrication is the control of contamination and foreign materials, e. g. that of drugs.

10. I was extremely worried about her, but this was neither the place nor the time for a lecture or an argument.

11. Differences between the social systems of states shall not be an obstacle to their approaches and cooperation.

12. I could describe the relations between our two countries as better, essentially franker, than I had ever known them.

13. In the near future flights going past Venus, and also Mars, will be offered with the development of science and technology.

14. The teachers find that students were easy to teach because they succeeded in putting everything they had been taught into practice.

15. The real reason why prices were, and still are, too high is complicated, no short discussion can satisfactorily explain this problem.

16. He was equally at home with the abstractions of number theory, the long calculations of astronomy and the practicalities of applied physics.

17. 白猫、黑猫，逮到耗子就是好猫。

18. 要改变这个厂的经济状况得花大力气。

19. 面对困难，坚定信心，依靠科技进步助推煤层气产业。

20. 多一点困难怕什么，封锁吧，封锁个十年、八年，中国的一切问题都解决了。

II. Choose a better translation.

1. These hospital expenses made inroads on their savings.

（A）医院的这些费用严重地消耗了他们的积蓄。

（B）我住院花的这些费用用掉了他们一半以上的积蓄。

（C）这些住院费耗掉了他们大部分积蓄。

（D）这些住院费耗掉了他们的积蓄。

2. He makes a good employer, as he was a good employee.

（A）他是个好老板，也是个好员工。

（B）他原先是个好员工，现在是个好老板。

（C）他制造好老板，正像他是一个好员工一样。

（D）他成为好老板，正如他是一个好员工一样。

3. His preoccupation with business left little time for his family.

（A）他全神贯注于事业，为他的家庭留下了很少的时间。

（B）他对事业的全神贯注留给他家庭的时间很少。

（C）他全神贯注于事业，因而能与家人共度的时间很少。

（D）他一心扑在事业上，所以留给家人的时间很少。

Unit 5　Translation Techniques（3）Omission

Omission is a technique opposite to amplification. What is regarded as a natural or indispensable element in one language may be regarded as superfluous or even "a stumbling block" in the other. Therefore, omission is necessary in translation practices.

1. Omission in English-Chinese Translation

Generally speaking, omission in English-Chinese translation is used to achieve succinctness, especially in dealing with excessive use of English pronouns and function words such as article, preposition, conjunction, *etc.*

1.1 Omission of personal pronouns and possessive pronouns

Pronouns are more frequently used in English than in Chinese. When translated into Chinese, many of them may be omitted so as to conform the rendering to Chinese usage.

（1）If **you** give **him** an inch, **he** will take a mile.

　　得寸进尺。

（2）He put **his** hands into **his** pockets and then shrugged **his** shoulders.

　　他将双手放进衣袋，然后耸了耸肩。

（3）They went into dinner. **It** was excellent, and the wine was good. **Its** influence presently had **its** effect on **them**. **They** talked not only without acrimony, but even with friendliness.

　　他们进入餐室用餐。美酒佳肴，顿受感染，言谈间不但没有恶言恶语，甚至还充满友好之情。

1.2 Omission of impersonal pronoun "it"

This case often occurs when "it" refers to something indefinite or without meaning.

（1）**It** was Pasteur who discovered that diseases are caused by living germs.

正是巴斯德发现疾病是由活着的病菌引起的。

（2）Let's make **it** 4 o'clock on Friday afternoon to have a talk in my office.

就让我们定为周五下午四点在我办公室谈吧。

（3）**It** was not until the 19th century that heat was considered as a form of energy.

直到 19 世纪人们才认识到热是能量的一种形式。

1.3 Omission of demonstrative pronouns and adverbs

（1）All **that** glitters is not gold.

发光的不一定都是金子。

（2）Oxygen by **which** fire burns is a colorless gas.

火焰借以燃烧的氧气是一种无色气体。

（3）Edison is a great inventor **whose** fame is world-wide.

爱迪生是个闻名世界的伟大发明家。

1.4 Omission of conjunctions

（1）Like charges repel each other **while** opposite charges attract.

同性电荷相斥,异性电荷相吸。

（2）Early to rise **and** early to bed makes a man healthy.

早起早睡身体好。

（3）Practically all substances expand **when** heated **and** contract **when** cooled.

几乎所有的物质都热胀冷缩。

（4）Never get on **or** off the bus before it comes to a standstill.

车未停稳，请勿上下车。

（5）This film showed how they put aside a thousand acres out west where the buffaloes roam **and** nobody can shoot a single one of them. **If** they do，they get in jail. It also showed some big National park with government airplanes dropping food down to the deer when they got snowed **and** had nothing to eat.

电影演的是他们怎么在西边那儿把一千亩土地划出，让水牛自由行动，谁也不准开枪打死一只。谁打死了，谁就得坐牢。有一段演的是某个大国立公园，政府派飞机注下扔吃的，（因为）那里的鹿让雪给封住了，没吃的。

1.5 Omission of articles

（1）Birds of **a** feather flock together.

物以类聚，人以群分。

（2）**The** water of **the** sea contains a considerable amount of salt.

海水中含有大量盐分。

（3）Any substance is made of atoms whether it is **a** solid，**a** liquid，or **a** gas.

任何物质，不论是固体、液体或气体，都由原子组成。

Note：Articles can't be omitted when they mean "一""每一""某一" or mean something important. For example：

Take the medicine three times **a** day. 每天服药三次。

1.6 Omission of prepositions

（1）Smoking **in** public places is prohibited.

公共场所禁止吸烟。

（2）Hydrogen is the lightest element **with** an atomic weight of 1.008.

氢是最轻的元素，原子量为 1.008。

（3）The products produced by this factory are good **in** quality and low **in** price.

该厂生产的产品物美价廉。

1.7 Omission of verbs

（1）When the pressure **gets** low，the boiling point **becomes** low.

气压低，沸点就低。

（2）These developing countries **cover** vast territories，**encompassing** a large population and abound in natural resources.

这些发展中国家地大物博，人口众多。

2. Omission in Chinese-English Translation

The technique of omission can also be used in Chinese-English translation，mostly in the following cases.

2.1 Omitting unnecessary repetition

（1）我曾经遇到过，不是氧气设备**出故障**，就是引擎**出故障**，或两者都**出故障**。

I had experienced oxygen and/or engine trouble.

（2）一个地方有一个**地方的全局**，一个国家有一个**国家的全局**，全世界有**全世界的全局**。

A locality has its own overall interests; a nation has another and the earth yet another.

（3）这种新药**缩短了**病人康复的时间，**减轻了**他的病痛，也**减少了**可能出现的严重副作用。

This new medicine improves the patient's recovery time, discomfort and possibly dangerous side effects.

2.2 Omitting classifiers and numerals of generalization

（1）电流的主要效应有磁效应、热效应和化学效应**三种**。

The chief effects of electric current are the magnetic, heating, and chemical effects.

（2）真空管的**五大**主要功能是：整流、放大、振荡、调制和检波。

The principal functions that may be performed by vacuum tubes are rectification, amplification, oscillation, modulation, and detection.

（3）刑事案件中以精神错乱为由进行辩护，这是一个涉及医学、法律和道德**三方面**的问题。

The issue of insanity as a defense in criminal cases is at the interface of medicine, law and ethics.

2.3 Omitting abstract category nouns

Sometimes when some nouns like "任务、工作、情况、问题、事业、局面、现象、性质" and so on do not indicate a specific notion but an abstract concept, omission is used here. For example：

（1）希望中东地区的人民早日结束社会动荡和纷扰不安的**局面**。

It is hoped that people in the Middle East areas can put an early end to the social unrest and upheaval.

（2）她的朋友们听到她家中的困难**情况**后，都主动伸出援助之手。

After her friends heard about the difficulties of her family, they offered her a helping hand.

（3）为了办好2014年北京亚太经合组织峰会，中国政府和人民做了大量的准备工作。

Chinese government and people have done a lot of preparations to ensure the success of the 2014 Beijing APEC summit.

2.4 Omitting detailed description

Occasionally, omission is used for the sake of succinctness, especially when the original Chinese is too meticulous.

（1）一到晚上，那个大公园里灯火辉煌，人语嘈杂，乐音悠扬，花草芬芳。

In the evening there are lights, chattering, music, and flowers in that big park.

（2）花园里面是人间的乐园，有的是吃不完的大米白面，穿不完的绫罗绸缎，花不完的金银财宝。

The garden was a paradise on earth, with more food and clothes than could be consumed and more money than could be spent.

（3）二百公里航道上遍布着无数险滩。险滩上，江流汹涌，回旋激荡，水击礁石，浪花飞溅，声如雷鸣。

Numerous shoals scattered over the 200km course give rise to many eddies. Pounding on the midstream rocks, the river roars thunderously.

Translation Practice

Ⅰ. Translate the following sentences, using the technique of omission.

1. The true joy of joys is the joy that joys in the joy of others.

2. Thermoplastic plastics become soft if they are heated.

3. He shrugged his shoulders, shook his head, cast up his eyes, but said nothing.

4. University applicants who had worked at a job would receive preference over those who had not.

5. The new computer is easy to operate, versatile, compact and has a pleasing modern design.

6. New forms of thought as well as new subjects for thought must arise in the future as they have in the past, giving rise to new standards of elegance.

7. This problem seems mostly effectively done by supporting a certain amount of researches not related to immediate goals but of possible consequences in the future.

8. But for many, the fact that poor people are able to support themselves almost as well without government aid as they did with it is in itself a huge victory.

9. The end of the short-lived age of fossil fuels is already in sight, soon in one or two centuries at the most we will have wasted all the world's resources of oil and coal.

10. Scientific exploration and the search for knowledge have given man the practical result of being able to shield himself from the calamities of nature and the calamities imposed by other men.

11. 21 世纪我们应该大力发展教育和科技事业。

12. 那位老人满脸皱纹，皮肤很黑，头发灰白稀疏。

13. 他这次旅行既有军事上的目的，又有政治上的目的。

14. 他们是白手起家的，他们需要人员，需要资金，需要场地。

15. 党和政府要依靠社会各方面的力量，加大对中西部地区的支持力度。

16. 我已经提前完成了交给我的工作，她也提前完成了交给她的工作。

17. 总之，就全国范围来说，我们一定能够逐步顺利解决沿海同内地贫富差距的问题。

18. 从一定意义上讲，中国的现代化建设离不开与世界各国的经济合作与贸易往来。

19. 大城市应该积极推进住房体制改革，加快建立城市贫困居民的最低生活保障制度。

20. 选择需要高深的思维功底，选择需要切合实际的判断能力，选择需要谨慎的态度，选择需要果敢的决断，选择需要充裕的时间。

Ⅱ. Choose a better translation.

1. They killed a bottle of *Erguotou* between them.

（A）他们二人喝光了一瓶二锅头。

（B）他们俩一起喝光了一瓶二锅头。

（C）他们在他们之间喝完了一瓶二锅头。

（D）他们二人对酌，把一瓶二锅头喝得一干二净。

2.　It would be one setback too many for him.

（A）这是一个对他来说太多的挫折。

（B）他可再也经不住什么挫折了。

（C）对他来说，这个挫折太大了。

（D）如果再有一个挫折，对他来说太多了。

3.　I hope we'll have got the instructions ready before you come tomorrow.

（A）我希望明天你来之前我们已经把说明书准备好了。

（B）我希望明天在你来之前可以把说明书准备好。

（C）我希望明天你来时，我们已把说明书都备齐了。

（D）希望我们把说明书准备好了以后，你再来。

Unit 6　Translation Techniques(4) Conversion

Conversion here refers to the change of parts of speech, of sentence elements and structures in translation.

1. Conversion of Part of Speech

1.1 Conversion of verbs

Since English is a static language and Chinese is a dynamic one, it is very common to see many different parts of speech in English will be translated into Chinese verbs, and Chinese verbs into English nouns, prepositions, adjectives or adverbs.

1) Noun ↔ Verb

(1) Your **presence** at the meeting will be a great support to our cause.

您**出席**会议将是对我们事业的极大支持。

(2) The **improvement** of energy efficiency in a restaurant will not only save money, but protect valuable natural resources, too.

提高餐厅的能源效率不仅能省钱，还能保护宝贵的自然资源。

(3) Although most people don't enjoy the **study** of grammar, its **mastery** can be extremely helpful in business.

虽然大多数人不喜欢**学习**语法，但在工作中，**精通**语法可能是非常有用的。

(4) 许多分析师们起劲地**宣传**谷歌公司的上市活动。

Many analysts have been the Google's biggest **boosters** for its public offering.

（5）大多数细菌不仅对人类无害，而且对**延续**地球上的一切生命都是绝对必要的。

Most bacteria are not only harmless to man but also absolutely essential to the **continuation** of all life on earth.

（6）太阳所**产生**的光和热需要每秒将六亿吨氢转化为氦。

The **output** of light and heat of the Sun requires that some 600 million tons of hydrogen be converted into helium in the Sun every second.

2）Preposition ↔ Verb

（1）Plants can't live **without** water and sunlight.

植物**离开**水和阳光就不能生存。

（2）The patient is now well and **off** medicine.

患者现已康复，**不需**服药了。

（3）No one has ever seen a single atom or molecule even **with** the most powerful microscope.

即使**用**倍数最大的显微镜，也没有任何人看到过单个的原子或分子。

（4）他**精通**好几门外语，如英语、法语、德语、俄语等。

He was **at home with** many foreign languages, like English, French, German, Russian, *etc.*

（5）氨是一种**具有**强烈刺激气味的无色气体。

Ammonia is a colorless gas **with** a very pungent odor.

（6）我们确实活得艰难，一要**承受**种种外部的压力，更要**面对**自己内心的困惑。

It's true that we have been leading a difficult life, for we need not only to be **under** various external pressures, but also to be **in the face of** internal perplexities.

3）Adjective ↔ Verb

Many English adjectives used after a link verb to indicate one's consciousness, feelings, emotions, desires, *etc.*, are always converted into Chinese verbs. These words include: confident, certain, careful, cautious, angry, sure, ignorant, afraid, doubtful, aware, concerned, glad, delighted, sorry, ashamed, thankful, anxious, grateful, able and so on. But it is just opposite in Chinese.

（1）This reform program is not **popular** with all of people.

并不是所有人都**喜欢**这个改革方案。

（2）A solar cell is **reproductive** by itself under any circumstances.

太阳能电池在任何情况下都可以**自行充电**。

（3）I am **aware** that Congress has passed the legislation on improving energy efficiency.

我**知道**议会已经通过了有关提高能源效率的立法。

（4）目前很多人**不了解**造成雾霾天气的真正罪魁祸首。

At present many people are **ignorant** of the real root of foggy weather.

（5）他们既**不向往**功名利禄，也不一味追求物质享受。

They are not **anxious** social climbers, and they have no devotion to material things.

（6）研究人员**确信**自己能研制出新的生产技术来提高煤炭的洁净利用。

Researchers are **confident** that they can develop a new technique to enhance the clean utilization of coal.

4）Adverb ↔ Verb

（1）I like Fridays **off**.

我喜欢每周五**休息**。

（2）When the price of land is **up**, that of housing will not fall.

地价**升高**，房价就不会下跌。

（3）经过仔细研究后，他们发现这个广告设计**落后**了。

After careful investigation they found the advertising design **behind**.

（4）为了避开交通拥堵，他每天日出之前就**起来**去上班。

Every day he is **up** before sunrise and goes to work in order to avoid the heavy traffic.

1.2 Conversion of nouns

1）Verb ↔ Noun

（1）He **directs** a research and development center.

他是研发中心的**主任**。

（2）These materials are **characterized** by good insulation and high resistance to wear.

这些材料的**特点**是：绝缘性好，耐磨性强。

（3）该设计的**目的**在于操作自动化，调节方便，维护简易，生产率高。

The design **aims** at automatic operation, easy regulation, simple maintenance and high productivity.

（4）中国新闻界纷纷**指责**美国某专题电视节目中使用的侮辱性语言。

There was a flood of **complaints** from the Chinese press about the insulting language used in one of America's special TV shows.

2）Adjective ↔ Noun

English adjectives with definite articles to indicate categories of people and things, or adjectives used as predicative to indicate the nature of things may also be converted into nouns.

（1）Both the compounds are acids, the **former** is strong, the **latter** weak.

这两种化合物都是酸，**前者**是强酸，**后者**是弱酸。

（2）It is a fact that glass is much more **soluble** than quartz.

事实上，玻璃的**可溶性**比石英大得多。

（3）刀具必须有足够的**强度、韧性、硬度**，而且要耐磨。

The cutting tools must be **strong, tough, hard**, and wear resistant.

（4）**高效、可靠**是电子计算机的主要优点。

Speed and **reliability** are the chief advantages of electronic computer.

3）Adverb ↔ Noun

（1）The old man is **physically** weak but **mentally** sound.

那位老人**身体**虚弱，但**心理**健康。

（2）Human translation will always be necessary for any text which is **stylistically** appealing and **semantically** complex.

对于任何**文体**引人入胜、**语义**复杂的文本，非得由人工翻译不可。

（3）这些部门的**思想工作**没有他们的**组织工作**做得好。

These departments have not done so well **ideologically** as **organizationally**.

（4）调查表明，估计该地区拥有资源**总量**为 300 万吨。

The investigation shows that **totally** 3,000,000 tons of resources have been calculated.

4）Pronoun ↔ Noun

（1）The specific resistance of iron is not so small as **that** of copper.

铁的电阻系数不如铜的**电阻系数**那样小。

（2）As the blood circulates through the kidneys, **they** separate certain waste materials to be eliminated.

血液流经肾脏时，**肾脏**分离出某些废物，将其排泄出去。

（3）健康比财富重要，因为**财富**不像**健康**那样带来那么多的幸福。

Health is above wealth, for **the latter** cannot give so much happiness as **that**.

（4）重量的单位是克，长度的**单位**是米，容积的**单位**是升。

The unit of weight is the gram, **that** of length is the meter, and **that** of capacity is the liter.

1.3 Conversion of adjectives

1）Noun ↔ Adjective

（1）He is a **stranger** to the operation of the electronic computer.

电子计算机的操作对他来说是**陌生**的。

（2）The absence of innovative researches is due to the growing **complexity** and widening scope of present study.

缺乏创新性研究是由于现代研究的内容越来越**复杂**，研究范围越来越广。

（3）地球上的生命依赖水而生存，而水是**不可替代的**。

Life on earth depends on water, and there is no **substitute** for it.

（4）希望即将在北京召开的亚太经合组织会议**圆满成功**。

It is hoped that the APEC meeting to be held in Beijing would be a **great success**.

2）Adverb ↔ Adjective

（1）Earthquakes are **closely** related to faulting.

地震与断裂运动有**密切**的关系。

（2）How can it be proved that gases are **perfectly** elastic?

如何证明气体具有**理想的**弹性呢？

（3）英语的变化很**微妙**，很**普遍**。

The English language had changed **subtly** and **pervasively**.

（4）电子计算机的**主要**特点是计算准确而迅速。

The electronic computer is **chiefly** characterized by its accurate and quick computation.

1.4 Conversion of adverbs

1) Adjective ↔ Adverb

（1）We place the **highest** value on our friendly relationship with developing countries.

我们**高度**珍视同发展中国家的友好关系。

（2）The boy has been a **puzzled** observer of the passenger's unusual movements.

那个小男孩一直**困惑不解地**观察着过注行人的不寻常举动。

（3）我们**仔细地**研究了这些化学元素的特性。

We have made a **careful** study on the properties of these chemical elements.

（4）水在4℃以下就**不断地**膨胀而不是**不断地**收缩。

Below 4℃, water is in **continuous** expansion instead of **continuous** contraction.

2) Noun ↔ Adverb

（1）The girl in the seat is studying the old woman beside her with **interest**.

座位上的那个女孩正**好奇地**打量着她旁边的那位老妇人。

（2）I have the **honor** to inform you that your application has been accepted.

我**荣幸地**通知阁下，您的申请已被接受。

（3）顾客们一致**愤怒地**谴责该商场的不道德行为。

Customers unanimously voiced their **indignation** to condemn the store's immoral acts.

（4）美国对日本**慢吞吞地**推进自由贸易进程感到不满。

The United States was unhappy with the **slowness** of Japan to advance free trade.

3) Verb ↔ Adverb

（1）I **succeeded** in persuading him to give up going abroad.

我**成功地**说服他放弃了出国的打算。

（2）Rapid evaporation at the heating surface **tends** to make the steam wet.

加热面上的迅速蒸发，**往往**使蒸汽的湿度变大。

（3）没人知道他要**离开**北京多久。

Nobody knows how long he will be **away** from Beijing.

（4）林则徐认为，要成功地制止鸦片买卖，就得**首先**把鸦片焚毁。

Lin Zexu believed that a successful ban of the trade in opium must be **preceded** by the destruction of the drug itself.

2. Conversion of Sentence Elements

Sometimes, conversion also involves the change of various elements of a sentence, such as from the subject to the object, and *vice versa*.

2.1 Conversion of the subject

1）Subject ↔ Predicate

（1）Mr. Gate's **marriage** will be next month.

盖茨先生将于下月**结婚**。

（2）应当始终**注意**保护计算机，使其免受各种病毒的袭击。

Care must be taken at all times to protect the computer from viruses.

2）Subject ↔ Object

（1）As the match burns, **heat and light** are given off.

火柴燃烧时发出**光和热**。

（2）A **stone** given a push along a rough road is quickly stopped by friction.

如果在粗糙路面上推一下**石头**，石头就会因摩擦而很快停止运动。

（3）我们知道，动植物的呼吸需要**氧气**。

We know that **oxygen** is necessary for the breathing of animals and plants.

（4）利用发电机可以把**机械能**再转变成电能。

The mechanical energy can be changed back into electrical energy by means of a generator.

3）Subject ↔ Adverbial

（1）His **illness** prevented him from attending the meeting.

由于生病，他没能来参加会议。

（2）**Darkness** released him from his last restraints.

在黑暗中，他就再也没有什么顾忌了。

（3）上周末**因为天气不好**，我们没去野营。

Bad weather prevented us from going camping last weekend.

（4）由于页岩气储量丰富，天然气价格一直处于低位。

An abundance of shale gas has helped to keep natural gas price low.

4）Subject ↔ Attributive

（1）**A semi-conductor** has a poor conductivity at room temperature, but it may become a good conductor at high temperature.

在室温下，**半导体的**电导率差，但在高温下，它却可能成为良导体。

（2）**各种材料的**磁特性差别很大。

Various substances differ widely in their magnetic characteristics.

2.2 Conversion of the predicate

Predicate ↔ Subject

（1）The statement was **phrased** in language unfamiliar to anyone who had listened to his speeches for years.

那个声明的**措辞**是多年来听他演讲的人都不熟悉的。

（2）令人吃惊的是，在这么盛大的晚会上那个顽皮男孩的**表现**相当不错。

It is surprising that the naughty boy **behaved** very well in such a big party.

2.3 Conversion of the object

1）Object ↔ Subject

（1）An automobile must have a **brake** with high efficiency.

汽车的**刹车**必须高度灵敏。

（2）Water has a **density** of 62.4 pounds per cubic foot.

水的**密度**是每立方英尺62.4磅。

2）Object ↔ Predicate

（1）The secretary cast impatient **glances** at the young man, and turned away without answering his question.

秘书不耐烦地**看了看**这个年轻人，转过头去，没有回答他的问题。

（2）尽管我们**失败**过，但仍要坚持下去。

We will preserve regardless of the past **failure**.

2.4 Conversion of the adverbial

1）Adverbial ↔ Subject

（1）In recent years, increasing attention has been paid to the economic benefit **in the production of our factory.**

近年来，我厂的生产越来越注重经济效益。

（2）我们社区附近没有大型购物中心。

There is no shopping mall **around our community.**

2）Adverbial ↔ Attributive

（1）The weather is warm and sunny **here.**

这里的气候温和，阳光充足。

（2）一线城市如北京、上海和广州的房地产特别昂贵。

The real estate is very expensive **in first-tier cities like Beijing, Shanghai and Guangzhou.**

3）Adverbial ↔ Predicate

（1）When a trademark owner applies for registration, the office will examine the application to see if the mark is **confusingly** similar to a mark previously registered or used.

当商标所有者申请注册时，商标局对该申请进行检查，看该商标是否**混淆**于以前注册或使用过的类似商标。

（2）他**接受了**医生的劝告，上星期退休以后立即做了眼科手术。

Acting on the advice of his doctor, he had his eye operated on right after he retired last week.

2.5 Conversion of the attributive

1）Attributive ↔ Predicate

（1）There is a large amount of energy **wasted** due to friction.

摩擦**消耗了**大量的能量。

（2）某些金属具有导电能力。

There are some metals **which possess** the power to conduct electricity.

2) Attributive ↔ Predicative

（1）The earth was formed from the **same** kind of material that makes up the sun.

构成地球的物质与构成太阳的物质是**相同的**。

（2）解决雾霾天气问题的确是**非常紧迫的**。

To solve hazy weather is indeed a most **pressing** problem.

3) Attributive ↔ Adverbial

（1）We should have a **firm** grasp of the fundamentals of computer science.

我们应该**牢固地**掌握计算机科学的基础知识。

（2）本书**生动地**再现了大庆油田石油会战的情景。

The book presents a **vivid** picture of Oil Battle in Daqing Oilfield.

3. Conversion of Sentence Structure

In translation, it is difficult to get rid of the influence of the source language structure. Thus, some changes of the sentence structures should be made as the followings.

1) Simple sentence ↔ compound or complex sentence

（1）Further delay would cause us greater losses.

我们如果再耽搁，将会蒙受更大的损失。

（2）His very appearance at any affair proclaims it a triumph.

任何场合，只要他一露面，就算成功了。

（3）She was a tall woman with a long nose and grey troubled eyes.

她个子挺高，长长的鼻子，一双灰色的眼睛，流露出忧郁的神情。

（4）他从来不谈家人，你不觉得奇怪吗？

Does it strike you as rather odd that he never talks about his family?

（5）只要小心谨慎，骑摩托车并不像一般人所想象的那样危险。

Careful cyclists are in less danger than is commonly believed.

（6）大街上静悄悄的，太阳火辣辣地照着，几乎看不见一个行人。

The main street was quiet and hot, almost deserted.

2) Complex sentence ↔ compound sentence

In English compound sentences, there are relations like cause and effect, condition and result, and time sequence. And English complex sentences have their marks such as those connectives, connective pronouns, connective adverbs, relative pronouns and relative adverbs. But many Chinese sentences do not have such connective devices. In translation, therefore, we should indicate such relations clearly.

(1) The snake catches the toad that eats the insect that nibbles the green leaves.

蛇吃癞蛤蟆，癞蛤蟆吃虫子，虫子吃绿叶。

(2) 你吃的粮食不是你种的，你穿的衣服不是你做的。

You don't grow the grain you eat and you don't make the clothes you wear.

3) Compound or complex sentence → simple sentence

(1) Inside pressure rises when temperature rises.

内部的压力随着气温的升高而升高。

(2) He is the one who would betray his friends any time.

他这种人随时都会出卖朋友。

(3) 职责所在，我不能临阵脱逃。

My duty forbids me to fly from danger.

(4) 人们通常反对使用血管扩张剂，可是并不反对使用氨茶碱。

Aminophylline does not share the usual objection to vasodilators.

4) Sentence with subject ↔ sentence without subject

(1) A little more care would have prevented such an accident.

如果当时稍加小心，就可避免这次事故了。

(2) The pricing and subsidy mode for wind and photovoltaic power generation is still a controversy because it lacks the market competition mechanism to encourage technological advance.

对于风电、光伏发电的定价补贴模式一直存在争议，这种模式缺乏鼓励技术进步的市场竞争机制。

(3) 全盘否定过去能源和电力体制改革的言论有失偏颇，不符合实际。

It is biased and unrealistic to negate the past energy and power reform.

(4) 加快天然气储气库建设，同时鼓励发展企业商业储备，有助于提高储气规模和应急调峰能力。

It will help to expand reserve scale and emergency peak shaving ability to accelerate the construction of natural gas storage tank while encouraging the development of commercial reserves in enterprises.

Translation Practice

I. Translate the following sentences, using the techniques of conversion.

1. We are enemies of all wars, but above all of nuclear wars.

2. To be a successful salesperson, you need to be a good listener.

3. It is impossible to live in society and be independent of society.

4. I recognized the absurdity of dealing with them through intermediaries.

5. The volume of trade has increased tremendously to the advantage of both China and Russia.

6. In the 1880s the United States was a land sharply divided between the immensely wealthy and the very poor.

7. After a certain point, when most of the relevant facts are in, you find yourself at the mercy of the law of diminishing returns.

8. When he catches a glimpse of a potential antagonist, his instinct is to win him over with charm and humor.

9. My reflection when I first made myself master of the central idea of the *Origin* was "How extremely stupid not to have thought of that!"

10. The Asia-Pacific region is characterized by a diversity of economic, social and political systems, cultural traditions and values, languages and aspirations.

11. The target to attack standard tests is wrong, for in attacking the tests, critics divert attention from the fault that lies with ill-informed or incompetent users.

12. 这份实验报告是依照说明书做的。

13. 他在讲话中特别强调提高产品质量。

14. 那个地区正在建设一座新的核电站。

15. 科学家们深信，所有物质都是不灭的。

16. 本文的目的在于讨论原材料和技术的新成就。

17. 众所周知，西方人与中国人的思维方式是不一样的。

18. 为了证实镭这种神秘物质，居里夫妇付出了辛勤的劳动。

19. 今天，信息时代已经取代了工业时代，并缩短了时间和距离。

20. 一位成功的科学家应善于观察、务求准确、具有耐心、客观求实。

21. 再深入研究产能改革和转型的关键推动力，我们会发现新趋势将会引领全球炼油行业未来的走向。

Ⅱ. Choose a better translation.

1. Unemployment has stubbornly refused to contract for more than a decade.

（A）十多年来，失业人数一直顽固地拒绝压缩。

（B）失业人数一直不下降，达十年之久。

（C）失业人数总是居高不下，已经十多个年头了。

（D）失业人数总是不收缩，这个问题已经持续十多年了。

2. Let a man learn as early as possible honestly to confess his ignorance, and he will be a gainer by it in the long run.

（A）尽早坦白承认自己的无知吧，这样就会长期受益。

（B）如果让一个人尽可能早地坦白承认自己的无知，从长远的观点来看，他会由此获益匪浅。

（C）让一个人尽可能早地学会坦白承认自己的无知吧。从长远的观点来看，他将通过这而成为得利者。

（D）让一个人尽早地学会承认他的无知吧。从长远的观点来看，这将使他得利。

Unit 7   Translation Techniques（5） Negation

As some linguists have pointed out, every language has its peculiarities in negation. And there are significant, though often neglected, differences between English and Chinese in negation—both in the way of thinking and in the mode of speaking.

For example, it is idiomatic to say "我认为他不对", "我想他不会接受邀请" in Chinese. In English, however, the same ideas would be expressed as "I don't think he is correct", "I don't think he will accept the invitation", with the negative shifted to the beginning of the sentence.

English negative words and expressions mainly fall into the following categories:

  * Full negatives: no, not, none, never, nothing, nobody, nowhere, neither, nor, *etc.*

  * Semi negatives: hardly, scarcely, seldom, barely, few, little, *etc.*

  * Partial negatives: not every, not all, not both, not much, not many, not always, *etc.*

  * Words with negative implication: fail, without, beyond, until, unless, lest, ignorant, refrain, refuse, neglect, absence, instead of, other than, except (for), rather than, more than, anything but, prefer... to, *etc.*

When translated into Chinese, these negative words and expressions should be adapted to idiomatic Chinese expressions.

1. Negation in English-Chinese Translation

1.1 Affirmative in English, negative in Chinese

Such cases are found in a wide range of expressions, words of different parts of speech, various phrases, or sentence structures.

(1) Your temper is **more than** I can bear. (conj.)

我忍受不了你的脾气。

(2) If it worked once, it can work twice. (sentence)

一次得手，再次不愁/一次成功，再次轻松。

(3) It was **beyond** his power to sign such a contract. (prep.)

他无权签订这样的合同。

(4) The days passed quickly, but she worked as **hard** as ever. (adv.)

日子很快过去了，但她工作上丝毫没有放松。

(5) You've got to **believe** in yourself, even when no one else does. (verb)

即使没人相信你了，你也不能对自己绝望。

(6) We cannot finish the work in the **absence** of these conditions. (noun)

在不具备这些条件的情况下，我们不能完成这项工作。

(7) We believe that the younger generation will prove **worthy of** our trust. (phrase)

我们相信，年青一代将不会辜负我们的信任。

(8) The next species of intelligent life on the earth will be a creature like ourselves but with a very large head and **weak** muscles. (adj.)

地球上下一代智能生命将是类似于我们人类的一种动物：头颅硕大，肌肉不发达。

1.2 Negative in English, affirmative in Chinese

This is just opposite to the previous cases.

(1) The machine has two serious **disadvantages**. (noun)

那台机器有两个严重缺陷。

(2) He is old, **none the less** he works like a young man. (phrase)

他虽然上了年纪，但干起活来，还像个年轻人。

(3) All the articles are **untouchable** in the museum. (adj.)

博物馆内的一切展品禁止触摸。

(4) Such flight couldn't long escape notice. (sentence)

这类飞行迟早会被人发觉。

(5) No one **but** a great philosopher could solve such a question. (conj.)

只有大思想家才能解决这样的问题。

(6) Many people agreed that the Prime Minister had in effect resigned **dishonorably**. (adv.)

许多人认为首相辞职实际上是很丢面子的。

(7) Her elder brother was an **indecisive** sort of person and always capricious when doing anything. (adj.)

她哥哥是个优柔寡断的人，而且做任何事情都反复无常。

(8) But then the two of you came into my world with all your curiosity and mischief and those smiles that never **fail** to fill my heart and light up my day. (verb)

后来，你们两个进入了我的世界，你们种种好奇的眼神、淘气的样子，还有微笑，总能填满我的心，照亮我的日子。

1.3 Same English words, either affirmative or negative in Chinese

(1) I'm new to the work.

这工作我是生手。（这工作我不熟悉。）

(2) He is free with his money.

他花钱大手大脚。（他花钱从不吝啬。）

(3) The subway station is no distance at all.

地铁站近在咫尺。（地铁站一点儿也不远。）

(4) He realized that he was in trouble.

他意识到自己遇到麻烦了。（他感到自己的处境不妙。）

(5) The computer was left intact, the money gone.

电脑还在，钱却不翼而飞了。（电脑原封未动，钱却不翼而飞。）

(6) She is just as rich as most of the girls who come out to Britain.

跟那些出国到英国去的女孩比一比，她不见得穷到哪儿去。（她跟那些出国到英国去的女孩一样富有。）

(7) He had not the least difficulty in discovering the true cause of his present be-

havior.

他很容易就弄清了造成他目前这般境况的真正原因。（对他来说，弄清造成自己目前这般境况的真正原因一点不难。）

（8）When the world was a simpler place, the rich were fat, the poor were thin, and right-thinking people worried about how to feed the hungry.

世界原本没有这么复杂，那时候富人胖，穷人瘦，头脑正常的人在发愁：怎样才能让挨饿的人吃上饭。（世界原本很简单，那时候富人胖，穷人瘦……）

1.4 Double negative for emphasis in English

Double negative in English, as in Chinese, is used for emphasis. In this case we may either drop both the negative words or keep the original depending on the idiomatic expression of the Chinese version.

（1）It never rains but pours.

不雨则已，雨必倾盆。

（2）They didn't praise him slightly.

他们对他大加赞赏。

（3）There is no rule that has no exception.

任何规则都有例外。

（4）I am not reluctant to accept your proposal.

我愿意接受你的建议。

（5）There is not any advantage without disadvantage.

有一利必有一弊。

（6）It is impossible but that a man will make some mistakes.

人不会不犯错误。（人人都会犯错误。）

1.5 Roundabout way of expressing the affirmative in English

This is an indirect way of expressing the strong emotion on the part of the speaker, and when translated into Chinese, the original mood should be properly kept.

（1）I couldn't feel better.

我觉得身体棒极了。

（2）He didn't half like the film.

他非常喜欢那部影片。

(3) If that isn't what I want to do!

我想做的就是这个呀！

(4) I couldn't agree with you more.

我太赞成你的看法了。

(5) He can't see his new roommate quick enough.

他很想尽快见到新室友。

1.6 Some traps in English negative structures

1) not... because：并不是因为，不……因为……

(1) The engine didn't stop because the fuel was finished.

引擎并不是因为燃料耗尽而停止运转。

(2) Don't scamp your work because you are pressed for time.

不要因为时间紧而敷衍塞责。

(3) She doesn't teach because she knows the answer to all questions.

她之所以教书并不是因为她知道所有问题的答案。

(4) She didn't attend the meeting because she wanted to.

她参加会议不是她自己想去的。

(5) Don't go for looks because they can deceive. Don't go for wealth, even that

fades away.

别倾心于容貌，因为容貌具有欺骗性；也别倾心于财富，因为财富也会

消散。

2) cannot... too/over/much：无论怎样……都不过分，应尽量，越……越好

(1) You cannot be too careful in driving.

开车时，越小心越好。

(2) That which is good cannot be done too soon.

好事做得愈快愈好。

(3) The importance of this conference cannot be overestimated.

这次会议的重要性无论怎么强调也不过分。

3) all/every... not：并非都

(1) Everything is not straightened out.

并非每一个问题都弄清楚了。

— 63 —

（2）All cities did not look like as they do today.

在过去，所有城市并不都像今天这样千篇一津。

（3）All that flatter you too much are not faithful friends.

捧你的人并非都是你的忠实朋友。

（4）All graduates will not be appointed to do some office works.

大学毕业生并非都被分配去做办公室工作。

4）both...not：两者不都

（1）But you see, we both cannot go.

但是我告诉你，我们俩不能同时都走。

（2）Both read the same Bible, and pray to the same God; and each invokes His aid against the other. The prayers of both could not be answered.

双方念的是同一本圣经，拜的是同一个上帝，但各方都要求上帝帮其去打倒对方。所以，双方的祈求不可能都得到满足。

5）It be + adj. + noun + that + negative sentence：再……也会

（1）It is a good workman that never blunders.

智者千虑，必有一失。

（2）It is a good athlete that never loses points.

没有常胜将军。

（3）It is a long lane that has no end.

路长必有弯，事久必有变。

2. Negation in Chinese-English Translation

2.1 Negative in Chinese, affirmative in English

（1）油漆未干！

Wet paint!

（2）他从不受贿。

He is above bribery.

（3）我完全没有成见。

I have a completely open mind.

（4）她的美丽无与伦比。

Her beauty is beyond compare.

（5）我没有注意到他的暗示。

His hint escaped me.

（6）他每天不预习就去上课。

He went to class before he prepared his lesson every day.

（7）卖方辩驳说，他卖这个价钱，已经是一分钱也不赚了。

The seller protests that the price he is charging is depriving him of all profit.

（8）白天一定要做的事，一定要说的话，现在都可不理。

All that one is obliged to do, or to say, in the daytime, can be very well cast aside now.

2.2 Affirmative in Chinese, negative in English

（1）那简直就是个奇迹。

That is nothing less than a miracle.

（2）但当时我脑子里却是一片空白。

But at the time I thought of nothing.

（3）他们工作时总是互相帮助。

They never work without helping each other.

（4）他实在轻率，竟当着她的面谈论此事。

It was inconsiderate of him to mention the matter in her hearing.

（5）这些细菌要在温度达到一百摄氏度时才会死亡。

These bacteria will not die until the temperature reaches 100°C.

2.3 Special negative Chinese expressions

（1）我认为他根本无法替自己的行为辩护。

I do not see at all how he can justify himself for such a conduct.

（2）我相信他们是不会反对你的建议的。

I don't believe that they will oppose your proposal.

（3）她一直认为自己比任何人干的活都多。

She never thought she could be outworked.

2.4 Translation of double negative

In this case, we can either keep original double negative or turn it into an affirmative expression.

(1) 我们必须不骄不躁，向人民学习。

We must be free from arrogance and rashness and learn from people.

(2) 她要是不说话，我还一直不知道她是外国人。

Until she spoke I had not realized she was a foreigner.

(3) 俗话说，"男儿有泪不轻弹，皆因未到伤心处"。

As the saying goes, "Men only weep when deeply hurt."

(4) 正如没经历过大事的人一样，他是经不起成功也经不起失败的。

Like those of little experience, he was easily elated by success and deflated by failure.

(5) 在我们准备一同在白宫开始新生活之际，我没有一天不为你们的忍耐、沉稳、明理和幽默而心存感激。

I am grateful every day for your patience, poise, grace, and humor as we prepare to start our new life together in the White House.

Translation Practice

I. Translate the following sentences, using the technique of negation.

1. If I had not repeated the mistake!

2. History has never been kind to Iraq.

3. I'll see you dead before that happens!

4. Not both the instruments are precision ones.

5. Both the instruments are not precision ones.

6. These constant changes in the weather beat me.

7. The significance of these incidents wasn't lost on us.

8. Slips are scarcely avoidable when you're new to your work.

9. Don't be above asking about things you do not understand.

10. I don't think we have asked for anything that they haven't done.

11. The problem cries out for a long-term, open-minded systematic research.

12. You couldn't turn on TV without seeing a woman demonstrating a product.

13. National universities, the pride of the prewar educational systems, were closed to women.

14. It is a valuable work. I do not think anyone writes so well that he cannot learn much from it.

15. The students hesitate when confronted with the vast untouched area of English vocabulary and usage which falls outside the scope of basic textbooks.

16. 我真看不懂这篇矿业论文。

17. 他开车时心不在焉，几乎闯祸。

18. 我到汽车站去接同学，可是没有接到。

19. 科学家不承认权威是真理的最后根据。

20. 那城市及周围的地方是不冻港和无核区。

21. 将来，石油再也不会是战争的一个祸根了。

22. 她觉得她再也不能忍受同学的讽刺、挖苦了。

23. 关于该地区的石油储量情况，人们一无所知。

Ⅱ. Choose a better translation.

1. She couldn't have come at a better time.

（A）她来得正是时候。

（B）她不能在一个更好的时间来。

（C）她本不能在一个更好的时候来。

（D）她不可能在这样好的时候出现。

2. In some poverty-stricken areas now, not a few people are found failing to achieve food security.

（A）现在在一些贫困地区，还有相当多的人被发现未达到食物安全。

（B）现在在一些贫困地区，许多人的食物还没有保障。

（C）现在在一些贫困地区，相当数量的人仍还没有解决温饱问题。

（D）现在在一些贫困地区，数量不少的人存在食品安全问题。

3. A causeless event or thing, we can not think of any more than we can of a stick with only one end.

（A）一件无缘无故的事情，我们能想到的就好似只有一头的棍子。

（B）一件无缘无故的事情是我们无法想到的，我们倒可以想到一根棍子只有一端。

（C）任何事情的发生都不可能是无缘无故的，正如一根棍子不可能只有一头一样。

（D）我们不可能设想有哪件事情是无缘无故发生的，就像我们不能设想有哪根棍子会只有一头一样。

Unit 8 Translation Techniques (6) Rendering of Passive Voice

The wide use of the passive voice is one of the outstanding features of English scientific documents. However, the passive voice is less commonly used in Chinese due to its flexible syntax. Therefore, conversion of voice is often necessary in English-Chinese and Chinese-English translation.

1. Passive Voice in English-Chinese Translation

1.1 Converting into active voice

1) Keeping the original subject

(1) Efficiency is usually expressed as a percentage.

效率通常用百分数来表示。

(2) In radiation, thermal energy is transformed into radiant energy, similar in nature to light.

在辐射时，热能转换成性质与光相似的辐射能。

(3) If you use firebricks round the walls of the boiler, the heat loss can be considerably reduced.

炉壁采用耐火砖可大大降低热耗。

(4) In pre - 2008, China was not expected to become the No. 1 energy-consuming economy until 2015, but it is now the major energy consuming nation.

根据2008年之前的预计，中国到2015年不会成为第一大能源消费国，但现在已成为主要的能源消费国。

2）Subject →object，prepositional object→subject

（1）Large quantities of fuel are used by modern industry.

现代工业耗用大量的燃料。

（2）About 10% of the world's oil supply is met by unconventional oils, and that number will increase.

非常规石油约占世界石油供给的10%，这一比例将持续攀升。

（3）Energy demand will be driven by developing nations and account for 93% of the new energy demand.

发展中国家的能源需求不断增加，占全球新增能源需求的93%。

（4）Global refinery construction continues to be driven by growth in the global demand for refined oil products.

全球对成品油的需求不断增长，促使世界各地不断建设炼油厂。

3）Adverbial →subject，subject →object

（1）Mean monthly rainfall in this city is shown in Table 3.1.

表3.1列出了该城市的月平均降水量。

（2）A film of oil is inserted between the sliding surfaces of a bearing.

轴承的滑动面之间上了薄薄的一层油。

（3）Accordingly, the successor phase-II exploration campaign was taken up during 2011—2012.

因此，2011—2012年期间开始了后续第二阶段的勘探活动。

（4）Communication satellites are used for international live transmission of the 29th Beijing Olympic Games throughout the world.

全世界都将通信卫星用于国际间第29届北京奥运会的实况转播。

4）Adding a general pronoun as the subject

（1）This steel alloy is believed to be the best available here.

人们认为这种合金钢是这里能提供的最好的合金钢。

（2）Rubber is found a good material for the insulation of cable.

人们发现橡胶是一种用于绝缘光缆的理想材料。

（3）If one or more electrons are removed, the atom is said to be positively charged.

如果原子失去一个或多个电子，我们就说该原子带正电荷。

（4）It has been calculated that the concentration of H$^+$ in water is 0. 0000001 gram per liter.

有人计算过，水中 H$^+$ 离子的浓度为每升 0. 0000001 克。

1.2 Changing into a predicative structure

（1）Electronics is based upon an understanding of physical world.

电子学是以人们对物质世界的认识为基础的。

（2）Many casting defects are caused by expansion properties of sand.

许多铸铁缺陷是由沙子的膨胀性质而引起。

（3）The high voltage section of the power supply is solid encapsulated.

电源的高压部分是固体密封的。

（4）Most primary highways are built and cared for by state governments.

大部分主要的公路都是由各州政府建造和管理的。

（5）Lead has been used as a material for sculpture since the time of early Greek.

铅是从古希腊开始用来作雕塑材料的。

1.3 Converting into subject-omitted sentences

（1）It has been proved that induced voltage causes a current to flow in opposition to the force producing it.

已经证明，感应电压使电流的方向与产生电流的磁场力方向相反。

（2）Russia and the Caspian Sea region are expected to export more gas to the East and West.

预计俄罗斯和里海地区将向东部和西部地区出口更多的天然气。

（3）An oxidation number may be assigned to each atom in a substance by the application of simple rules.

应用一些简单的规则，可以给一种物质里的各个原子指定氧化值。

（4）Efforts have been identified significant coking coal resources in a number of different areas within the Zambezi River Basin.

经过努力，已经确定了在赞比西河流域的许多不同区域有着大量的焦煤资源。

1.4 Keeping passive voice in Chinese with "被……" "遭……" "受……" "为……所" "加以……"

（1）With the emergence of an electronic currency, every one of us would be affected.

随着电子货币的出现，我们每一个人都会受到影响。

（2）Sustainable management is seen as a practical and economical way of protecting species from extinction.

可持续管理被人们视为一种保护生物物种使之免于灭绝的实用又经济的办法。

（3）The moon, as well as the stars and the sun, is made use of by the mariner to find his latitude and longitude at sea.

月亮与星星和太阳一样，常被海员用来确定在海上的经纬度。

（4）For a better understanding of the present invention, two embodiments will now be described by way of example, with reference to the accompanying drawings.

为了更好地理解本发明，两个实施方案现通过举例和附图加以说明。

1.5 Replacing by other structures

In many cases, however, passive voice in English cannot be rendered into good Chinese by means of the patterns mentioned above. Therefore, it is up to the translator to adjust or remold the whole structure, so as to bring out a proper and readable Chinese version. For example:

（1）He had been wedded to translation.

他与翻译工作结下不解之缘。

（2）Most trees are denuded of leaves in winter.

大多数树木冬天要落叶。

（3）The news was passed on by word of mouth.

众口相传,消息不胫而走。

（4）She was delivered of a girl of 7 *Jin* this August.

今年 8 月份她生下了一个 7 斤重的女孩。

（5）The village is populated by about 5000 farmers.

这个村子里住着大约 5000 个农民。

（6）Not too much can or should be read into the percentages.

这些百分比不能说明太多的问题，也不应利用它们来说明太多的问题。

(7) Each payment to be made hereunder shall be made in U. S. dollars.

本协议中的各项支付必须用美元。

(8) She and her husband were asked out for the wedding banquet of their friends last Sunday.

上周日她和丈夫应邀赴朋友的婚宴去了。

2. Passive Voice in Chinese-English Translation

Passive structures are less often used in Chinese than in English, so Chinese-English translation is mainly from the active voice to the passive voice. Generally, the Chinese passive structures can be classified into two patterns: sentences with or without the passive labels.

2.1 Chinese sentences with passive labels

In translating such sentences, we may copy the English passive structure.

（1）他深受大家的尊敬，被选为执委会主席。

He is respected by all and was elected Chairman of the executive committee.

（2）窗上的玻璃让那个孩子打破了，他一定要挨骂的。

The window pane was broken by the child; he will certainly be scolded.

（3）我们的对外政策受到全世界人民的支持。

Our foreign policy is supported by the people all over the world.

（4）特别是 2011 年实现了非常规油气资源勘探的重大突破，延长石油集团被列为我国首批 40 个矿产资源综合利用示范基地之一。

Especially in 2011, an important breakthrough was made in the exploration of unconventional oil and gas, therefore Yanchang Petroleum Group was listed as one of China's first 40 demonstration bases of comprehensively utilizing mineral resources.

However, not all Chinese sentences with passive labels should be translated into English sentences with passive voice, especially when it comes to English intransitive verbs.

（1）老太太被风吹病了。

The old lady fell ill because of the draught.

（2）天太冷，水管都给冻住了。

It was so cold that the water pipes froze.

2.2 Chinese sentences without passive labels

Sometimes sentences of this category seem to be active in structure, but actually passive in meaning.

（1）征集论文的通知现正陆续发出。

A call for papers is now being issued.

（2）应当注意机器的工作温度。

Attention must be paid to the working temperature of the machine.

（3）这种杀虫剂效果良好，屡试不爽。

This new insecticide has been proved effective every time it is used.

（4）地铁15号线于2014年底建成。

The construction of subway line 15 was completed at the end of 2014.

（5）新型晶体管的开关时间缩短了2/3。

The switching time of the new-type transistor is shortened two thirds.

（6）同时，建成了聚丙烯等重点项目，实现从"单一燃料型"向"燃料化工型"的成功转型。

Meanwhile, polypropylene and other major projects were established, realizing the successful transformation from the mode of "single fuel" into "chemical fuel".

2.3 Some Chinese expressions in common use

Some Chinese expressions may be conveniently translated into English by using the pattern "It be + p.p. + that clause".

（1）应该说，局势基本上是稳定的。

It should be said that the situation is basically stable.

（2）必须指出，有些问题还需要澄清。

It must be pointed out that some questions have yet to be clarified.

（3）众所周知，火药是中国古代的四大发明之一。

It is well known that gunpowder is one of the four great inventions of ancient China.

（4）有人预测，电脑和网络技术之间新的互动将会对未来的工业产生巨大的影响。

It is estimated that the new interaction between computers and Net technology will have significant influence on the industry of the future.

Similar structures we have

It is asserted that... 有人主张 ……

It is believed that... 有人认为……

It is generally considered that... 大家(一般人)认为……

It will be said... 有人会说……

It was told that... 有人曾经说……

It can't be denied that... 大家认为……

It is said that... 据说……

It is hoped that... 希望……

It is learned that... 据闻……

It is reported that... 据报道……

It is supposed that... 据推测……

It must be admitted that... 必须承认……

It will be seen from this/that... 由此可见……

It may be said without fear of exaggeration that... 可以毫不夸张地说……

Translation Practice

Ⅰ. Translate the following sentences, paying attention to the conversion of the voice.

1. At least two quarts of water is required daily by a normal individual.

2. Crude mineral ores and crude oil must be purified before they can be used.

3. It is estimated that these tropical forests contain anything from 50 to 90 percent of all animal and plant species on earth.

4. Those who support the "nature" side of the conflict believe that our personalities and behavior are largely determined by biological factors.

5. Satellites, however, must be closely watched, for they are constantly being tugged at by the gravitational attraction of the sun, moon and earth.

6. Over the years, tools and technology themselves as a source of fundamental innovation have largely been ignored by historians and philosophers of science.

7. Mineral oil is useful only when it is cleaned and separated into different commercial products. These products can be used for ships, trains, cars and airplanes.

8. And it is imagined by many that the operations of the common mind can be by no means compared with the processes of scientists, and that they have to be acquired by a sort of special training.

9. New sources of energy must be found, and this will take time, but it is not likely to result in any situation that will restore that sense of cheap and plentiful energy we have had in the times past.

10. The method of scientific investigation is nothing but the expression of the necessary mode of working of the human mind: it is simply the mode by which all phenomena are reasoned about and given precise explanations.

11. On the whole such a conclusion can be drawn with a certain degree of confidence, but only if the child can be assumed to have had the same attitude towards the test as the other with whom he is being compared, and only if he was not punished by lack of relevant information which he possessed.

12. Some are deceived into thinking that people like to store up energy, to rest and save themselves as much as possible. Just the opposite. It is energy expenditure that is satisfying. Expending energy, in a sense, creates its own replacement—there is no reservoir such that the more you use the less you have.

13. 势能可以很容易地变为动能。

14. 大家知道，氢是最轻的元素。

15. 解决电机发热问题的办法终于找到了。

16. 用煤和石油可以制成各种各样有用的东西。

17. 应该鼓励各地方政府尽快出台保护环境和提高能源效率的办法。

18. 应当调整高校的专业设置，改进教学方法，以适应社会的需要。

19. 一切科技成就都是建立在理性思维的基础之上，没有理性思维就不能有科学。

20. 石油供应可能随时被切断；不管怎样，以目前这种石油消费速度，只需 30

年左右，所有的油井都会枯竭。

Ⅱ. Choose a better translation.

1. True friendship is like health, the value of which is seldom known until it is lost.

（A）真正的友谊就像健康一样，其价值要到失去以后才体验到。

（B）真正的友谊就像健康一样，它的价值直到失掉还很少被知道。

（C）真正的友谊就像健康一样，失掉了才觉得宝贵。

（D）真正的友谊就像健康一样，其价值失掉了才有人知道。

2. Companies with a big staff in Beijing find themselves squeezed between high operating costs and shrinking business.

（A）在北京，员工庞大的公司发现自己受着高运行成本和萎缩业务两方面的挤压。

（B）在北京，员工队伍庞大的公司面临运行成本高，业务不断缩减的局面，日子颇不好过。

（C）北京的一些员工队伍庞大的公司承受着运行成本高和业务不断缩减的双重压力，颇感处境艰难。

（D）北京的一些员工队伍庞大的公司腹背受敌，运行成本越来越高，业务不断萎缩。

Unit 9　Translation Techniques（7）
Rendering of Subordinate Clauses

1. Substantive Clauses

English subordinate clauses are classified into six groups, namely, subject clauses, object clauses, predicative clauses, appositive clauses, attributive clauses, and adverbial clauses. Since the first four of them function as nouns in a complex sentence, they are generally called substantive clauses. This section is going to focus on some specific methods of translating English substantive clauses.

1.1 Subject clauses

For those subject clauses introduced by such pronouns as "what, whoever, how, that, when", *etc.*, we can keep the original order in translating.

(1) Why he refused to cooperate with you is still a mystery.

他拒绝和你一起合作的原因还是个谜。

(2) Whoever wants to join our club for environmental protection can sign here.

任何想加入我们环保俱乐部的人都可以在这儿签名。

(3) What was once regarded as impossible has now become a reality.

过去认为不可能的事现已变成了现实。

(4) That he became a lawyer may have been due to his father's influence.

他能成为一名律师很有可能是源于他父亲的影响。

When "it" functions as a formal subject, we can ignore "it," or turn "it" into a phrase placed at the beginning of or in the middle of the sentence, or into a sentence placed at the end.

（1）It isn't so much what he works: the question is whether he works at all.

他干什么并不重要，问题是他到底有没有干。

（2）It is obvious that most countries of the world have a strong desire to mutually expand their trade.

显然，世界上大多数国家都强烈地希望扩展彼此之间的贸易。

（3）Nowadays it is a well-known fact that second-hand smoking does even more harms to human health.

二手烟对人类健康危害更大，这在今天已经是无可争辩的事实。

（4）It is almost unbelievable that a fish is able to generate electricity strong enough to light small bulbs, even to run an electric motor.

几乎令人难以置信的是，鱼能发电，而且发出的电力足以点亮小灯泡，甚至能开动马达。

1.2 Object clauses

Generally speaking, there is no need to change the order when translating object clauses. However, in some cases, for example, when "it" functions as the formal object in a complex sentence, we can ignore it, keep or change the order when necessary.

（1）I regard it as an honor that I am chosen to attend the international conference.

我被选去参加国际会议，感到十分荣幸。

（2）I take it for granted that he is well qualified but needs more experience.

我想当然地认为，他完全够条件但还需要更多的经验。

（3）Science does not mean believing and remembering what other people tell us.

科学并不意味着相信并记住前人积累的间接经验。

（4）I explained to the boss that I could not finish my work on time since my computer was down.

我跟老板解释说，我的计算机坏了，所以不可能按时完成工作。

1.3 Predicative clauses

English predicative clauses are generally translated in the original order. For example:

（1）The current problem is which is the effective way to lower the housing price.

目前的问题是哪种方法能有效降低房价。

（2）It seems that these two branches of science are mutually dependent and interacting.

看来这两个科学分支是相互依存、相互作用的。

（3）In communications, the problem of electronics is how to convey information from one place to another.

在通信系统中，电子学要解决的问题是如何把信息从一个地方传递到另一个地方。

1.4 Appositive clauses

An appositive clause is a clause that, functioning as a noun, stands in apposition to a noun. The following methods are usually used.

1) Treat the appositive as an attributive, i. e. , putting the appositive clause before the noun

（1）The concept that we have to work at happiness comes as news to many people.

对很多人来说，我们需要努力感受幸福的这种说法可能是前所未闻的。

（2）The fact that he got the first prize of National Energy and Technology Progress Award pleased everybody.

他荣获国家能源科技进步一等奖的事实令大家都很开心。

（3）Behaviorists, in contrast, say that differences in scores are due to the fact that blacks are often deprived of many of the educational and other environmental advantages that whites enjoy.

相反，行为主义者认为，成绩的差异是由于黑人往往被剥夺了白人在教育及其他环境方面所享有的许多有利条件这一事实。

2) Use punctuation marks or other means

Punctuation marks such as colon, dash, or such expressions as "这样", "这种", "这一", "即", *etc.* are used for stress. The appositive clause can be placed either before or after the noun.

（1）But considering realistically, we had to face the fact that our prospects were less than good.

但是现实地考虑一下，我们不得不正视这样一个事实：我们的前景并不美妙。

（2）The fact that the gravity of the earth pulls everything towards the center of the earth explains many things.

　　地球引力把一切东西都吸向地心，这一事实解释了许多现象。

（3）Not long ago the scientists made an exciting discovery that this "waste" material could be turned into plastics.

　　不久以前，科学家们有了一个令人振奋的发现，即可以把这种"废物"变为塑料。

3）Change the structure of the sentence

（1）An order has been given that the researchers who are now in the skylab should be sent back.

　　已下命令将现在航天实验室里的研究人员送回来。

（2）Even the most precisely conducted experiments offer no hope that the result can be obtained without any error.

　　即使是最精确的实验，也没有希望获得无任何误差的实验结果。

（3）However, the writing of chemical symbols in the form of an equation does not give any assurance that the reaction shown will actually occur.

　　但是，将化学符号写成反应式，并不意味着所表示的反应确实会发生。

1.5 Chinese complex sentences

The concept of substantive clauses does not exist in Chinese syntax. But we have complex sentences: combined sentences（联合复句）and a sentence containing a modifier（偏正复句）. They are different from English complex sentences in that the former is often combined by several short sentences and the latter by strict rules with sentences embedded in one another. Therefore, in Chinese-English translation, we often translate clusters of short and brief Chinese sentences into long and overlapped English sentences.

（1）在她的眼皮底下，儿子一天天长大起来：看着他蹒跚学步，咿呀学语，逐渐懂事，她天天惊喜不已。

　　She watched her son grow and develop day by day and it was a never-ending wonder as he began to walk, talk and reason.

（2）他停下脚步，转过身来，定睛一看，原来是个上了年纪的妇女：身材修长，虽然饱经风霜，显得有点憔悴，但风韵犹存。

　　It was an old woman, tall and shapely still, though withered by time, on whom his eyes fell when he stopped and turned.

（3）中国的风力设备制造是在引进国外技术基础上发展起来的，技术的先进性、零部件的可靠性、生产人员的素质、管理环节的严格性都存在差距。

China's wind power equipment manufacturing is developed on the basis of the introduction of foreign technology, so there is a big gap in terms of advanced technology, reliable parts and components, quality of production staff and rigid management.

Translation Practice 1

I . Put the following sentences into Chinese, paying attention to the subordinate clauses.

1. It is evident that a well lubricated bearing turns more easily than a dry one.

2. The behaviorists maintain that, like machines, humans respond to environmental stimuli as the basis of their behavior.

3. That our environment has little, if anything, to do with our abilities, characteristics and behavior is central to this theory.

4. Supporters of the "nature" theory insist that we are born with a certain capacity for learning that is biologically determined.

5. The belief that something permanent transcends us and that our existence has some larger meaning can help us be happier.

6. Nowadays it is understood that a diet which contains nothing harmful may result in serious disease if certain important elements are missing.

7. Galileo's greatest glory was that in 1609 he was the first person to turn the newly invented telescope on the heavens to prove that the planets revolve around the sun rather than around the Earth.

8. The assertion that it was difficult, if not impossible, for a people to enjoy its basic rights unless it was able to determine freely its political status and to ensure freely its economic, social and cultural development was now scarcely contested.

9. It is not a question how much a man knows, but what use he can make of what he knows; not a question of what he has acquired, and how he has been trained, but of what

he is, and what he can do.

10. 随着社会经济发展对资源、环境的需要，能源安全涵盖的内容日益多元化。

11. 当前，我国产业结构不尽合理，重化工业比重偏大，消耗了我国约 61% 的电力资源。

12. 我厂生产的床垫工艺先进，结构新颖，造型美观，款式多样，舒适大方，携带方便。

13. 实现我国煤层气产业快速发展的当务之急是迅速提高科技水平，提高单井产量，释放产能。

Ⅱ. Choose a better translation.

1. You are posted in what had preceded all this, but I was not.

（A）你现在是知道了这以前的原委的，可是我当时并不知道。

（B）你现在已了解了发生在这以前的事，可当时我并不知道。

（C）你现在已经明白了这件事的全部原委，但我当时却全然不知。

（D）你现在已了解了发生在这以前的事，可当时我却被蒙在鼓里。

2. It is a rule never to be forgotten that whatever strikes strongly, should be described while the first impression remains fresh upon the mind.

（A）有一条原则永远也不能忘记：无论什么印象深刻的东西都应该在第一印象深刻时进行描述。

（B）凡是印象深刻的东西，就应该趁最初印象记忆犹新的时候，加以描述，这是必须记住的一条原则。

（C）永远也不能忘记这样一条原则：无论什么印象深刻的东西都应该在第一印象深刻时进行描述。

（D）这是一条不能忘记的原则：凡是印象深刻的东西都应该在第一印象深刻时进行描述。

2. Attributive Clauses

English attributive clauses are usually complicated and long. There are two kinds of attributive clauses: restrictive and non-restrictive ones. An English sentence may be followed by an unlimited number of attributive clauses that stand on the right side of the word being modified, while a Chinese sentence allows only a limited amount of words preceding the word being modified. For example：

（1）This is the cat.

这是那只猫。

（2）This is the cat that killed the rat.

这就是那只捕杀了老鼠的猫。

（3）This is the cat that killed the rat that ate the cheese.

这就是那只捕杀了偷吃了奶酪的老鼠的猫。

（4）This is the cat that killed the rat that ate the cheese that lay in the house.

这就是那只捕杀了偷吃了放在房间里的奶酪的老鼠的猫。

（5）This is the cat that killed the rat that ate the cheese that lay in the house that Jack built.

这就是那只捕杀了偷吃了放在杰克修建的房间里的奶酪的老鼠的猫。

Apparently, Chinese version （3）, （4）and （5）seem very awkward because all the information can't be put into a single sentence. Therefore, readable versions should be somewhat like the following：

（3）这就是那只捕杀了老鼠的猫。老鼠偷吃了奶酪。

（4）这就是那只捕杀了老鼠的猫。老鼠偷吃了堆放在屋里的奶酪。

（5）这就是那只捕杀了老鼠的猫。老鼠偷吃了堆放在屋里的奶酪。屋子是杰克盖的。

The following methods can be adopted in translating English attributive clauses.

2.1 Restrictive attributive clauses

1）Combination

It means placing attributive clause before the word being modified (the antecedent), with the aid of Chinese pattern of "……的……".

（1）Air pollution is a pressing problem which we must deal with.

大气污染是我们必须解决的一个迫切问题。

（2）During construction, problems often arise which require design changes.

在施工过程中，常会出现需要改变设计的问题。

（3）Engineering is the profession that puts scientific knowledge to practical use.

工程学是一门将科学知识运用于实践的专业。

（4） This training program provides companies with the knowledge and skills which are needed for their success.

本培训课程为各公司提供取得成功所需的必要知识和技能。

2） Division

It means dividing the sentence in two, placing the attributive clause after the principal clause and repeating or omitting the antecedent being modified.

（1） Galileo was a famous Italian scientist by whom the Copernican theory was further proved correct.

伽利略是著名的意大利科学家，他进一步证明了哥白尼学说是正确的。

（2） Today we live in a world where American firms no longer have automatic technological superiority.

如今在我们生活的世界中，美国公司已不再自然而然地具有技术上的优势。

（3） Very wonderful changes in matter take place before our eyes every day to which we pay little attention.

非常奇异的物质变化每天都在眼前发生，这是我们几乎没有注意到的。

（4） There will be television chat shows hosted by robots, and cars with pollution monitors that will disable them when they offend.

届时，将出现由机器人主持的电视谈话节目以及装有污染监控器的汽车，一旦这些汽车排污超标，监控器就会使其停驶。

3） Amalgamation

It means combining the meanings of the principal clause and the attributive clause in a single Chinese sentence, usually for "there be..." pattern. Besides, there are some English complex sentences in which emphasis is laid on the attributive clause. In this case, the principal clause may be condensed into the subject of a simple sentence, taking the attributive clause as its predicate. For example:

（1） There are some metals which possess the power to conduct electricity and the ability to be magnetized.

有些金属既能导电，又能被磁化。

（2） There are events taking place at this time which dim our hopes and lessen the prospects.

目前发生的一些事情使我们觉得希望渺茫，前途暗淡。

（3）Good clocks have pendulums which are automatically compensated for temperature changes.

好的钟摆可以自动补偿温度变化造成的误差。

2.2 Non-restrictive attributive clauses

1）Division

* Translated into compound sentences by repeating the antecedents

（1）The molecules exert forces upon each other, which depend upon the distance between them.

分子之间存在着力的作用，该力的大小取决于它们之间的距离。

（2）The most important form of energy is electrical energy, which is widely used in our daily life.

最重要的能源形式是电能，它广泛地应用于我们的日常生活。

（3）The team member gave us a detailed introduction about the process of the research, which is very important to us.

项目组人员向我们详细介绍了研究过程，这对我们来说非常重要。

* Translated into compound sentences by omitting the antecedents

（1）The lungs are subjected to several diseases which are treatable by surgery.

肺易受几种疾病的侵袭，但均可经手术治疗。

（2）When I try to understand what it is that prevent so many Americans from being as happy as one might expect, it seems to me that there are two causes, of which one goes much deeper than the other.

为什么如此多的美国人不能如想象中那样幸福呢？我认为有两个原因，而且有深浅之分。

* Translated into independent sentences

（1）Nevertheless the problem was solved successively, which showed that the computations were accurate.

不过，问题还是逐一得到了解决。这说明计算是准确的。

（2）I received the impression of a brutal, clever, competent man who, in business matters, at all events, would be pitiless.

我对这个人的印象是又残酷又精明能干。这种人在生意上无论何时都毫无怜悯之心。

（3）Engineers have had a direct role in the creation of most of modern technology——the tools, materials, techniques, and power sources that make our lives easier.

工程师在绝大部分现代科技创新中发挥着直接的作用。例如，为使生活更加便捷，我们靠他们才有了工具、材料、技术和能源。

2）Combination

（1）The tree, the branches of which are almost bare, is a willow.

那棵树枝几乎光秃的树是柳树。

（2）Transistors, which are small in size, can make previously large and bulky radios light and small.

体积小的晶体管使得先前那种大而笨的收音机变得又轻又小。

2.3 Attributive clauses functioning as adverbials

Sometimes, attributive clauses are not limited to the meaning of the nouns they modify, but somewhat like adverbials, so attributive clauses are not always translated into attributive clauses in Chinese. They should be translated according to the habit of Chinese language.

1）Translated into Chinese adverbial clauses of cause

（1）To make an atomic bomb we have to use uranium 235, in which all the atoms are available for fission.

制造原子弹，我们必须用铀235，因为铀235的所有原子都会裂变。

（2）There is a steady shift of scientists from the pure to the applied field, where there are more jobs available, frequently more highly-paid and with better technical facilities.

科学家不断从理论科学研究领域转移到应用科学研究领域，因为后者能够提供更多的工作机会，而且通常待遇优厚，技术设施好。

（3）American's basic fear is of the slack up of protectionism, and above all, its capital outflow which to them means job outflow.

令美国人最恐慌的是放松贸易保护主义的做法，尤其害怕资本外流，因为对他们来说，资本外流就等于工作机会外流。

2）Translated into Chinese adverbial clauses of result

（1）She seeks happiness in selfish enjoyment, where it can never be found.

她在自私的享乐中寻求幸福，结果是永远也找不到幸福。

（2）There was something original, independent, and heroic about the proposal that pleased all of judges.

这个提案富于创造性，别出心裁，很有魄力，所以评委都很喜欢。

（3）Solar energy is a clean and renewable power resource on the earth, which is widely used for generating electricity.

太阳能是地球上的一种清洁的可再生能源，因此被广泛用于发电。

3）Translated into Chinese adverbial clauses of concession

（1）The recent actions of North Korea, which have aroused universal disapproval of the world, are not given up by them.

尽管朝鲜近日的行动已激起全世界的普遍反对，但他们并没有放弃。

（2）Electronic computers, which have many advantages, cannot carry out creative work and replace man.

尽管电子计算机有许多优点，但是它们不能进行创造性工作，也不能代替人。

4）Translated into Chinese adverbial clauses of condition

（1）The same thing, which happened in the old society, would amount to disaster.

同样的事情，如果是发生在旧社会，就等于是灾难。

（2）There is an optimum size for the reactor at which the chain reaction will just work.

想要链式反应能够有效地工作，反应堆就必须有一个最合适的尺寸。

（3）Anyone who thinks that rational knowledge need not be derived from perceptual knowledge is an idealist.

如果认为理性知识可以不从感性知识得来，这个人就是个唯心主义者。

5）Translated into Chinese adverbial clauses of purpose

（1）Chinese trade delegations have been sent to European countries, who will negotiate trade agreements with respective governments.

中国派出一些贸易代表团出访欧洲各国，以便同各国政府洽谈贸易协议。

（2）Workers have to oil the moving parts of the machine, the friction of which may be greatly reduced.

工人们必须给机器的转动部件加油，以便大大减少这些部件间的摩擦。

(3) Currently, every country in the world has trade barriers, which are designed to protect its economy against international market forces.

如今世界各国都设置了贸易壁垒，以保护本国经济免受国际市场力量的冲击。

6) Translated into Chinese adverbial clauses of time

(1) The thief, who was about to escape, was caught by the policemen.

小偷正要逃跑时，被警察抓住了。

(2) Electrical energy that is supplied to a lamp can be turned into light energy.

电供给电灯时，就会变成光能。

2.4 Attributive elements in Chinese

In Chinese, there is no attributive sentence but it is quite common to see long attributive with "的" pattern. When translating, such long structure can be transformed into English attributive phrase, or clause, or an independent sentence.

(1) 全世界的科学家都在寻找净化空气、防止空气受到各种有害工业废气污染的有效方法。

The scientists everywhere in the world are looking for efficient methods to make the air clean and protect it from pollution by all kinds of harmful industrial waste gases.

(2) 在我们肉眼看来似乎静止不动的一杯水中却有数不清的水分子正在进行着大量的无规则的热运动。

Although the water in a glass (which) looks to be totally motionless to our naked eyes, a great deal of thermal movement of its countless molecules is going on disorderly inside.

(3) 当前我们迫切需要有一个装备优良、人员齐备、按照安全保护原则、本着一丝不苟的精神建立起来的先进核能实验室。

A well-equipped and well-manned nuclear energy lab is badly needed at present. Such a lab, of course, must be advanced in technology and built in accordance with the principle of security as well as in the spirit of meticulous discretion.

（4）数以百万计的美国人尽管从来不认为自己会违反法津，却正在越来越随便地践踏那些专为保护和造福于社会而制定的法规。

Millions of Americans who would never think of themselves as lawbreakers are taking increasing liberties with the legal codes that are designed to protect and nourish their society.

Translation Practice 2

I. Translate the following sentences, paying attention to the attributive clauses in English and the "……的……" pattern in Chinese.

1. He likes Miss Nancy, who despises him.

2. A man is nothing who yields his purpose.

3. They turned a deaf ear to our demands, which enraged all of us.

4. He is a man respected by people, who is always thinking of others.

5. Many people insist on buying another house, which they have no use for.

6. He wishes to write an article, which will attract public attention to the air pollution in this city.

7. There was another man who seemed to have much experience in teaching Bible, and that was Dr. Stephenson.

8. You compare her with your English-women who wolf down from three to five meat meals a day and naturally you find her a sylph.

9. While at a museum, one can frequently rent a small recording machine that will explain the objects on display as you move through the museum.

10. Now the integrated circuit has reduced by many times the size of the computer of which it forms a part, thus creating a new generation of portable minicomputers.

11. In office, figures, lists and information are compiled, which tell the managers or heads of the business what is happening in their shops or factories.

12. Unlike global warming and ozone depletion—which, if the political will was there, could be reduced by cutting gas emission—preserving bio-diversity remains an intractable problem.

13. Behaviorists suggest that the child who is raised in an environment where there are

many stimuli which develop his or her capacity for appropriate responses will experience greater intellectual development.

14. The increasing speed of scientific development will be obvious if one considers that TV, space craft, and nuclear-powered ships, which are taken for granted now, would have seemed fantastic to people whose lives ended as recently as 1920.

15. There is nothing more disappointing to a hostess who has gone to a lot of trouble or expense than to have her guest so interested in talking politics or business with her husband that he fails to notice the flavor of the coffee, the lightness of the cake, or the attractiveness of the house, which may be her chief interest and pride.

16. 一个不怕困难、百折不挠、坚持到底的科学工作者一定会在科研工作中取得光辉的成就。

17. 这一条约实际上是将荷兰法学家雨果·格劳秀斯（Hugo Grotius）在 1609 年所说的世界上的海洋是属于一切人的这一名言尊为至理。

18. 过去，我们的企业一般不重视经济效益，广泛存在着劳动无定员、生产无定额、质量无检查、成本无核算的现象，造成人力、物力、财力的很大浪费。

II. Choose a better translation.

1. I haunted all the meetings in London where debates followed lectures.

（A）伦敦的集会，凡是演讲结束以后接着进行辩论的，我都参加。

（B）我参加所有在伦敦举行的讲演以后就是辩论的集会。

（C）我参加所有在伦敦的集会，在那里，讲演以后接着就是辩论。

（D）我经常参加伦敦的集会，因为讲演之后都有辩论。

2. Many people spoke highly of Hakassia's soil, which was rich, and slightingly of its climate, which was unsettled and dry.

（A）很多人都推崇哈卡斯的土壤，而不满意它的气候；哈卡斯的土地肥沃，可是那儿的气候变化多端而且干旱。

（B）很多人都推崇哈卡斯的土地土壤好，它肥沃；不恭维它的气候，因为变化多端而干燥。

（C）很多人都推崇哈卡斯肥沃的土壤，而不满意它那变化多端而干燥的气候。

（D）很多人都高度评价哈卡斯肥沃的土壤，而贬低其变化多端而干燥的气候。

3. Adverbial Clause in English-Chinese Translation

English adverbial clauses include adverbials of time, place, cause, condition, concession, purpose, result and so on, and their sentence structures are flexible. The basic translation principle is to arrange them in an order of subordinate clauses first and principal ones last, and omit some unnecessary conjunctive words, while adding connectives when necessary and rearranging the order according to the logic in translating Chinese adverbial clauses into English. Besides, sometimes those adverbial clauses can be interchanged in translating, such as from adverbial clause of time into that of place.

3.1 Adverbial clauses of time

1) Expressing time relations by lexical means

(1) Ice keeps the same temperature while melting.

冰在溶化时, 其温度保持不变。

(2) After he had completed the experiment, he got the results published in a key journal.

实验完成后, 他把实验结果发表在了一本核心期刊上。

(3) Engineers face the challenging task of keeping pace with the latest advances while working to shape the technology of the future.

在致力于未来技术发展的同时, 工程师还面临着跟上最新技术发展的挑战。

2) Translated into Chinese adverbial clauses of condition

(1) Turn off the switch when anything goes wrong with the machine.

如果机器发生故障, 就把电门关上。

(2) A body at rest will not move till a force is exerted on it.

若无外力的作用, 静止的物体不会移动。

3.2 Adverbial clauses of place

English adverbial clauses of place can also be translated into Chinese adverbial clauses of condition.

(1) The materials are excellent for use where the value of the work pieces is not high.

如果零件价值不高, 最好使用这些材料。

(2) Generally, air will be heavily polluted where there are factories.

一般来讲，哪里有工厂，哪里的空气污染就会严重。

3.3 Adverbial clauses of cause

1）Translated into corresponding Chinese clauses with "因为""由于" and so on

(1) As the moon's gravity is only about 1/6 the gravity of the earth, a 200-pound man weighs only 33 pounds on the moon.

由于月球的引力只有地球引力的六分之一，所以一个体重200磅的人在月球上仅有33磅重。

(2) Because science and technology are progressing and changing so rapidly, today's engineers must study throughout their careers to make sure that their knowledge and expertise do not become obsolete.

因为科学技术在飞速发展和变化，如今的工程师必须毕生不断学习以确保其知识和专业技能不过时。

2）Translated into Chinese principal clauses

In this case, the principal clauses are turned into clauses of result by having "所以" *etc.* before them.

(1) Pure iron is not used in industry because it is too soft.

纯铁太软，所以不用于工业。

(2) Since information is continuously sent into the system as it becomes available, teletext is always kept up-to-date.

随着新获得的资料不断输入，所以电传系统总是保持最新信息。

3.4 Adverbial clauses of condition

1）Translated into Chinese adverbial clauses of condition, or clauses of supposition

(1) Provided that there is no opposition, we shall build nuclear power station here.

如果没人反对，我们就在这里建核电站了。

(2) Should there be urgent situation, press the red button to switch off the electricity.

万一有紧急情况，请按红色按钮以切断电源。

(3) A body can move uniformly and in a straight line, there being no cause to change that motion.

如果没有改变物体运动的原因，那么物体将作匀速直线运动。

2）Translated into Chinese supplementary clauses

（1）Any body above the earth will fall unless it is supported by an upward force equal to its weight.

地球上的任何物体都会落下来，除非它受到一个大小与其重量相等的力的支持。

（2）Humans should be able to use any species of animal or plant for their benefit, provided enough individuals of that species are left alive to ensure its continued existence.

人类为了自身利益可以使用任何动物或植物物种，前提是能使每一物种有足够的个体存活下来，从而确保该物种得以延续其生存。

3.5 Adverbial clauses of concession

1）Translated into corresponding Chinese adverbial clauses of concession

（1）Though the task was difficult, they managed to accomplish it in time.

虽然任务艰巨，但他们还是设法及时完成了。

（2）I don't think you'll be able to understand this formula even when you finish college education.

即使你大学毕业了，我认为你也不会明白这个公式的意思。

2）Translated into Chinese "unconditional" clauses such as "不管""不论"，*etc.*

（1）He got the same result whichever way he did the experiment.

不论用什么方法做实验，他所得到的结果都相同。

（2）All living things, whether they are animals or plants, are made up of cells.

一切生物，不管是动物还是植物，都是由细胞组成的。

3.6 Adverbial clauses of purpose

Adverbial clauses of purpose, when translated into Chinese, may either be placed before or after the principal clause of the sentence.

（1）Steel parts are usually covered with grease for fear that they should rust.

钢制零件通常涂上润滑脂，以防生锈。/为了防锈，钢制零件通常需涂上润滑脂。

（2）A rocket must attain a speed of about five miles per second so that it may put a satellite in orbit.

火箭必须获得每秒大约五英里的速度，以便把卫星送入轨道。/ 为了能把卫星送入轨道，火箭必须获得每秒大约五英里的速度。

3.7 Adverbial clauses in Chinese-English translation

Considering different features in hypotactic English and paratactic Chinese, it is up to the translators to detect the implied meaning of the Chinese sentence and bring it out in English version. The following are some typical examples.

（1）她不老实，我不能信任她。

Since she is not honest, I cannot trust her.

（2）打肿脸充胖子，吃亏的是自己。

If you get beyond your depth, you'll suffer.

（3）向上的力与向下的力相等，气球就保持在这一高度。

The force upward equals the force downward so that the balloon stays at the level.

（4）开发油气资源是生产活动、经济活动，政府不宜随意干预。

Developing oil and gas resources is a productive and economic activity, so it shouldn't be interfered arbitrarily by the government.

（5）没有完善的技术服务市场，走"众人拾柴火焰高"发展道路只是句空话。

The development path that "many hands make light work" would mean nothing if there were no perfect technical service markets.

（6）与此同时，对能源资源环境的约束增强，经济发展受到更多制约，中国必须把能源安全作为战略的重中之重。

Meanwhile, due to the further restrictions on energy resources and environment as well as more constraints on economic development, China must take energy security as a strategic priority.

Translation Practices 3

Ⅰ. Translate the following sentences, paying attention to the adverbial clauses.

1. Electricity is such a part of our everyday lives and so much taken for granted nowa-

days that we rarely think twice when we switch on the light or turn on the radio.

2. Until such time as mankind has the sense to lower its population to the point where the planet can provide a comfortable support for all, people will have to accept more "unnatural food".

3. These facts will remain true whether we are dealing with the application of psychology to advertising and political propaganda, or of medical science to the problem of overpopulation or old age.

4. Sometimes, tests do not compensate for gross social inequality, and thus do not tell how able an underprivileged youngster might have been had he grown up under more favorable circumstances.

5. 电是一种非常重要的能量，没有它，现代化工业就不能发展。

6. 一条新的定理必须经过实践的检验以后，才能肯定它是否有价值。

7. 在阅读科学材料时，常常需要一读再读。你应该一边阅读，一边参照所有的图表和图片。

8. 我们把自主创新作为未来发展的主要驱动力，走出一条资源节约、环境友好、社会和谐的可持续发展道路。

Ⅱ. Choose a better translation.

1. As the desert is like a sea, so is the camel like a ship.
（A）正如沙漠像海，因此骆驼就像一只船。
（B）如果说沙漠像大海，那么骆驼就像航行在大海上的一只船。
（C）沙漠似海，骆驼似舟。
（D）由于沙漠跟大海一样，所以骆驼就等同于海上的船。

2. It was quite a few years before he finally finished his novel.
（A）过了好几年，他才终于写完了这本小说。
（B）在他最后完成这本小说之前，已经是好几年了。
（C）在他最终完成这本小说之前，又是好几年。
（D）他最终完成了小说，但那是好几年以后的事了。

Unit 10   Translation Techniques (8) Rendering of Long Sentences

Translation of a typical long English/Chinese sentence usually consists of two stages and seven steps as follows.

Stage I: Comprehension

Step 1: drafting a skeleton of the long sentence;

Step 2: inferring the main idea from the context;

Step 3: distingwishing between the principal and subordinate elements;

Step 4: finding out the interrelations between principal and subordinate clauses.

Stage II: Presentation

Step 1: Entering on a tentative translation of each sentence division;

Step 2: Rearrangement and synthesis;

Step 3: Finishing touches.

Let's analyze the above seven steps in the following illustration.

It is nothing else than impurities parentally inherent in ore that seriously affect the quality of the latter, which is formed as a result of geological vicissitudes including diastrophic movement, eruption of volcano, sedimentation, glaciation and weathering *etc.*, under the action of which phylogenic rocks, volcanic complex, aqueous rocks, sedimentary rocks *etc.*, come into being, some of which exist in a stage of symbiosis, the main cause of the absence of pure rocks in nature, wherein lies the reason for the need of separation technology and apparatus, namely, ore-dressing devices and equipment, so far impotent to meet the requirements of metallurgical industry the scientists make every endeavor to elevate to a new high by laser separation.

矿石是由地质变化形成的，这些地质变化包括地壳变迁运动、火山爆发、沉积作用、冰川作用和风化作用等。在上述地质变化的作用下，形成了火成岩、火山杂岩、水成岩和沉积岩等。正是岩石中的天然固有杂质影响了矿石的质量。上述这些岩石中，有些处于共生状态——这也是自然界没有天然纯矿石的主要原因。人们之所以需要矿石分离技术与器械，即选矿装置与设备，其原因盖出于此。迄今为止，分离技术和器械尚远不能满足冶金工业的需要，科学家们正全力以赴，利用激光分离机把冶金工业提高到一个新水平。

1. Long Sentence in English-Chinese Translation

1.1 Following the original order

（1）The proportion of various ingredients which go into concrete, the way it is mixed, and even the water which is used are very important to the finished material.

制作混凝土所用的各种配料的比例、搅拌的方法，乃至所用的水，对成品材料来说都是十分重要的。

（2）Engineers should be curious about the "how" and "why" of natural and mechanical things and creative in finding new ways of doing things, and able to analyze problems systematically and logically and to communicate well.

工程师应该对自然和机械事物的方式和方法充满好奇心，能够创造性地发现开展工作的新方法，能够有步骤、有逻辑地分析问题，并善于沟通交流。

（3）You have all heard it repeated that men of science work by means of induction and deduction that by the help of these operations, they, in a sort of sense, manage to extract certain natural laws from the Nature, and that out of these by some special skill of their own, they build up their theories.

你们都多次听说过，科学家是用归纳法和演绎法工作的，他们用这种方法，在某种意义上说，力求从自然界找出某些自然规律，然后，他们根据这些规律，用自己的某种非同一般的本领，建立起他们的理论。

1.2 Reversing the original order

（1）Does it really help the society, the victim, or the victim's family, to put in jail a man, who drove a car while drunk, has injured or killed another person?

一个人酒醉后开车，压死或压伤了另一个人，就将这个人关进监狱，这样做对社会、受害者或受害者的家庭是否真的有好处呢？

（2）The high-quality wind power equipment couldn't be produced without the solid theoretical foundation, qualified materials and equipment, necessary test and practices.

如果没有扎实的理论研究基础、没有合格的材料和设备、没有必要的试验和实践基础，很难生产出合格的风力设备。

（3）Global operating rates of refineries may trend downward if there are not delays in projects scheduled to come on stream in the 2014—2015 timeframe, which, based on the history of refinery project development, is quite likely.

从炼油厂项目的发展历史来看，如果 2014—2015 年预计投入生产的项目不延迟，全球炼油厂的运营率可能会有所下降。

1.3 Breaking up

（1）Plastics is made from water which is a natural resource, coal which can be mined through automatic and mechanical process at less cost and lime which can be obtained from the calcination of limestone widely present in nature.

塑料是由水、煤和石灰制成的。水是天然资源；煤是用自动化和机械化的方法开采的，成本较低；石灰是由燃烧自然界中广泛存在的石灰石得来的。

（2）Aristotle could have avoided the mistake of thinking that women have fewer teeth than men, by the simple device of asking Mrs. Aristotle to keep her mouth open while he counted.

亚里士多德误认为妇女牙齿的数目比男人少。这种错误，他本来是可以避免的，而且办法很简单。他只要请亚里士多德夫人把口张开，他亲自数一数就行了。

（3）Human beings have distinguished themselves from other animals, and in doing so ensured their survival, by the ability to observe and understand their environment and then either to adapt to that environment or to control and adapt it to their own needs.

人类把自己和其他动物区别开来。与此同时，人类还具有观察和了解周围环境的能力。他们要么适应环境，要么控制环境，或根据自身的需要改造环境。人类就这样一代代地生存下来。

1.4 Inserting marks like dash, bracket

(1) Of all languages, English has the largest vocabulary, perhaps as many as two million words, and one of the noblest bodies of literature.

在所有语言中，英语的词汇量最大——大约200万单词——也是具有最丰富的文学宝库的语言之一。

(2) If you go to visit Nobel's old residence, the house in which the great chemist remained a bachelor throughout his life, you will catch sight of a shelf laden with experimental records.

如果你参观诺贝尔的故居——在那座房子里，这位伟大的化学家过了一辈子的独身生活——你将会看到一个堆满实验记录的书架。

(3) The need to produce goods and services at quality levels previously thought impossible to obtain in mass production and the spreading use of participatory management techniques will require a work torce with much higher levels ot education and skills.

提供高质量产品和服务的需要（而过去则认为大批量生产是不可能做到的）以及参与型管理技术的推广使用，都对劳动力提出了更高的教育和技术要求。

1.5 Recasting according to logic and Chinese habit

(1) Dr. Smith resumed the activities of anti-cancer experiment begun in 1945 and financed by the Federal government as soon as he snapped from his original disappointment at repeated failures, which had resulted in its forced suspension.

史密斯医生于1945年开始着手由联邦政府资助的抗癌实验。他由于屡遭失败而感到沮丧，被迫终止了实验工作。现在他又重新振作起来，恢复了抗癌实验活动。

(2) It has been more than one year since Alfred Jackson, a 38-year-old Brooklyn plumber, was shot and killed by a neighbor because Mr. Jackson wanted to park

in the spot where the man was walking his dog.

　　阿尔弗莱德·杰克逊，38 岁，生前是布鲁克林一个水暖工人。有一天他想在邻居遛狗的地方停放汽车，竟被邻居开枪打死。这件事发生已有一年多了。

（3）But without Adolf Hitler, who was possessed of a demoniac personality, a granite will, uncanny instincts, a cold ruthlessness, a remarkable intellect, a soaring imagination and—until toward the end, when drunk with power and success, he overreached himself—an amazing capacity to size up people and situations, there almost certainly would never have been a Third Reich.

　　然而，如果没有阿道夫·希特勒，那就几乎可以肯定不会有第三帝国。因为阿道夫·希特勒有着恶魔般的性格、花岗石般的意志、不可思议的本能、无情的冷酷、杰出的智力、深远的想象力以及对人和时局惊人的判断力。这种判断力最后由于权力和胜利冲昏了头脑而自不量力，终于弄巧成拙。

2. Long Sentence in Chinese-English Translation

Long sentence translation is also a headache for the translator in Chinese-English translation. Since there is a great disparity between Chinese and English sentence structures, we should learn to tackle them discriminatingly. The usual methods adopted in translating long Chinese sentences into English include the change of clause order and division/breaking up. For example:

（1）"十五" 期间要突出重点，搞好开局，着重加强基础设施和生态环境建设，力争五到十年内取得突破性进展，同时使科技、教育有较大发展。

　　During "the Tenth Five-Year Plan" period, we need to place emphasis/stress on key projects for a good beginning of the program. Construction of infrastructure and protection of the ecological environment should take priority, and we should strive for major breakthroughs within five to ten years. At the same time, we hope to develop science, technology, and education considerably.

（2）中国是世界上最大的发展中国家，中国政治、社会稳定，经济持续发展，市场将更加开放，市场环境不断改善，这将给包括欧盟企业在内的国际工商界带来更多的投资、贸易机会。

　　As the largest developing country in the world, China is proved to have stable political and social environment, constant economic growth and ever-opening market as well as ever-better market atmosphere, which is going to generate more investment and trade opportunities for international business circles including EU businesses.

（3）一些大型电力集团公司将业务延伸到了设备制造，并要求本集团公司投资的风电场主要采用本企业生产的风力设备，这不仅造成了不公开的竞争环境，而且不利于风电产业的持续、健康发展。

Some large power groups expand their businesses to equipment manufacturing, and require the group's investment in the wind farms by using their own equipment, which not only causes the closed competitive environment, but also damages the sustained and sound development of the wind power industry.

（4）我们不但要有一个农林牧副渔布局合理、全面发展、能够满足人民生活和工业发展需要的发达农业，还要有一个门类齐全、结构合理、能够满足社会消费和整个国民经济发展需要的先进工业。

Version 1: We need not only a developed agricultural system with a rational distribution and all-round development of farming, forestry, animal husbandry, side-line production and fishery, meeting the needs of the people's life and expanding industry, but also an advanced industrial system which is complete in range and rational in structure and which meets the needs of consumers and the expansion of the whole national economy.

Version 2: We need not only a developed agricultural system but also an advanced industrial system. The former requires a rational distribution and all-round development of farming, forestry, animal husbandry, side-line production and fishery to meet the needs of the people's life and expanding industry, while the latter should have a complete range and a rational structure to meet the needs of consumers and the expansion of the whole national economy.

Translation Practices

I. Translate the following long sentences, paying attention to their structure.

1. Such is human nature in the West that a great many people are often willing to sacrifice higher pay for the privilege of becoming white collar workers.

2. The late 1960s offered case after agonizing case of brash young go-go entrepreneurs who put together glittering conglomerates they had no idea how to manage.

3. It is not that the scale in the one case, and the balance in the other, differ in the principles of their construction or manner of working but that the latter is a much finer apparatus and of course much more accurate in its measurement than the former.

4. The method was largely developed by physicists, chemists and biologists; it was later adopted by people working in such areas as education, psychology and sociology, where the subjects of research were often people.

5. There are several reasons why Kissinger no longer appears to be the magician the world press had made him out to be, an illusion which he failed to discourage because, as he would admit himself, he has a tendency toward megalomania.

6. We have a feeling in retrospect, amounting to a practical belief that we could have left undone the things that we have done, and that we could have done the things that we ought to have done and did not do, and we accuse or else excuse ourselves accordingly.

7. There is just the same kind of difference between the mental operation of a man of science and those of an ordinary person as there is between the operations and the methods of a baker or a butcher weighing out his goods in common scales, and the operations of a chemist in performing a difficult and complex analysis by means of his balance and finely graduated weights.

8. As a resort, conditions permitting, we may seek at home medical service, namely, diagnosis and treatment from abroad, to use professional terminology, telesatdiag, as compared with vis-à-vis consultation, say, in an ill-equipped, poorly staffed hospital, particularly on an acute, severe or, in physician's view, unidentified case, undoubtedly a most effective therapeutic device available.

9. The secret of the moon remained unveiled until the latter half of the twentieth century due to the lack of lunar space carrier, for a series of questions concerning fuel, material, safe landing, propelling mechanism and particularly electronic computation, *etc.* were too intricate to solve under the technical conditions early in this century, which have since been undergoing profound change and greatly improving.

10. 历史业已证明，人类对于资源的认识、开发和利用，以及利用资源制造生产工具的能力，是社会生产力发展水平的重要标志，也在一定程度上决定了一定的社会基本结构和发展形态。

11. 矿产资源是自然资源的重要组成部分，是人类社会发展的重要物质基础。新中国成立 60 多年来，矿产资源勘查开发取得巨大成就，探明一大批矿产资源，建成比较完善的矿产品供应体系，为中国经济的持续、快速、协调、健康发展提供了重要保障。目前，中国 92% 以上的一次能源、80% 的工业原材料、70% 以上的农业生产资料来自于矿产资源。中国高度重视可持续发展和矿产资源的合理利用，把可持续发展确定为国家战略，把保护资源作为可持续发展战略的重要内容。

II. Choose a better translation.

1. Born in 1879 in Ulm, Germany, Albert Einstein was two years old when his parents moved to Munich, where his father opened a business in electric supplies.

（A）阿尔伯特·爱因斯坦于 1879 年出生在德国的乌尔姆城。在他两岁的时候，随父母移居慕尼黑。他父亲在慕尼黑开了一家工厂，从事电气器材的生产与销售。

（B）阿尔伯特·爱因斯坦 1879 年生于德国的乌尔姆城，当他父母移居慕尼黑并在那里开了一家生产电气器材的工厂时，他才两岁。

（C）阿尔伯特·爱因斯坦 1879 年生于德国的乌尔姆城。他父母移居慕尼黑并在慕尼黑开了一家生产电气器材的工厂，当时他两岁。

（D）阿尔伯特·爱因斯坦 1879 年生于德国的乌尔姆城。2 岁时，他随父母移居慕尼黑，在那里他父亲开了一家生产电气器材的工厂。

2. We still have problems—plenty of them. But it's just plain wrong, unjust to our country and unjust to our people, to let those problems stand in the way of the most important truth of all: Chinese living environment is on the mend.

（A）我们还有问题——而且有大量问题。但是，如果让这些问题妨碍一个最重要的事实——中国人的生存环境正在好转，那就是完全错误的，对我们的国家不够公正，对我们的人民亦不够公正。

（B）我们还存在问题——而且问题很多。但是中国人的生存环境正在好转。如果我们让问题挡住了视线而看不见这样一个最重要的事实，那就是完全错误的，无论对我们的国家和人民都有失公正。

（C）我们仍然还有问题，而且是大量的。但是如果让这些问题站在所有重要事实的道路中间，那简直是错误的，对我们的国家和人民都不公正：中国人的生存环境正在好转。

（D）我们还有很多问题。但是，因为这些问题我们就忽略一个最重要的事实——中国人的生存环境正在好转，那就大错特错了，而且对我们的国家和人民都不够公正。

Part II General Description of Scientific Literature
Unit 11 Introduction to Scientific Literature

Literature is a set of work on a particular subject, printed material, esp. giving informatio, the body of writings on a particular subject (scientific literature).

1. Classification of Literature

There are various literatures such as textbooks, monographs, papers, encyclopedias, periodicals and special documentation covering patent documents, copyrights, contracts/agreements, reports, conference papers, dissertations (or theses), product specifications, proposals, technical archives, electronic hypertexts, *etc.*

2. Linguistic Features of Scientific Literature

2.1 In terms of style

Scientific literature is a kind of formal writing, avoiding all colloquial expressions. For example, "establish, gradually, terminate, verify" are used instead of "build/set up, step by step, end/finish, prove/bear out".

2.2 In terms of syntax

It has rigorous grammatical structure, and in most cases is rather unitary. Frequently used are indicative sentences, imperative sentences, complex sentences, long sentences, the relative pronoun "that" or "which", "It be + adj. (past participle) + that ..." sentence patterns and passive voice, *etc.*

2.3 In terms of morphology

Scientific literature is featured in high specialization, the use of technical terms and jargons, unambiguous implication, fixed sense of words, more compound words, Latin and Greek words, contracted words, noun clusters, *etc.*

2.4 In terms of rhetoric

Unlike literary English (LE), English for science and technology (EST) writings seldom employs such literary rhetorical devices as hyperbole, figures of speech, personification, antithesis, irony, humour, *etc.* Look at the following two passages which all describe man but by different devices of expression.

EST

Man is metazoan triploblastic chordate vertebrate pentadactyle mammalian eutherian primate, hominid homo. The main outlines of each of his principal systems of organs may be traced back like those of other mammals to the fishes.

人类归属于脊索动物门类、脊椎动物亚门类、哺乳纲、真兽亚纲、灵长目、人科、人属。他是后生的三胚层五趾动物，其每一个主要器官系统的轮廓都像其他哺乳动物一样，可以追溯到鱼类。

LE

What a piece of work is a man! How noble in reason! How infinite in faculty! In form and moving how expressive and admirable! In action how like the angel! In apprehension how like a god! The beauty of the world! The paragon of animals!

人类是一件多么了不起的杰作！多么高贵的理性！多么伟大的力量！多么优美的仪表！多么文雅的举动！在行为上多么像一个天使！在智慧上多么像一个天神！宇宙的精华！万物的灵长！

Besides, non-verbal language is also very popular in various scientific literatures such as signs, formulas, charts, tables, photos, *etc.* for the sake of accuracy, brevity, and clarity.

3. Translation of Scientific Literature

Different scientific literatures may have different linguistic features although documentary works of various kinds do have similar characteristics in common. Therefore, we should treat the translation of each kind of documentary work discriminatingly. For example, translating the patent documents requires stereotyped expressions and formal patterns. Copyright works usually call for rigid grammar; whereas legal documents, contracts and agreements are characterized by their strict grammar and syntax, as well as their formal styles. And in the translation of proposals and reports, the matter-of-fact-attitude is of chief concern.

Translation Practice

Put the following passage into Chinese / English.

1. As an important means for preserving knowledge, various literatures have become precious resources or treasures for the mankind, which have greatly contributed to the social progress of the human race.

Professional literatures have been regarded as "intangible assets" of the whole world because they are, on the one hand, the summary, generalization, and development of the achievements obtained on the basis of previous experiences or studies; and on the other hand, they have been accumulated and handed down from generation to generation. In this sense, therefore, all kinds of literature are records of precious research findings and academic achievements, and the crystallization of human civilization.

2. 科技文献是用文字、图形、符号、声频和视频等方式记录人类科学技术知识的载体，是人类文明的产物。科技文献具有四大功能，即信息承载功能、知识体现功能、创新支撑功能和教育培训功能。科技文献资源是一个发展着的动态体系。由于科技突飞猛进的发展，其综合与分化的趋势日益明显，使得科技文献呈现出数量激增，老化加速，类型复杂，形式与内容广泛、分散、交叉、渗透的状况。

Unit 12   Scientific Literature（1）
Patents and Copyrights

1. Patents

A patent is the short form of a patent right. It is a kind of exclusive rights of an inventor granted in accordance with law. Therefore, a patent can be defined as an official record of specific rights awarded to an individual or group to prevent others from copying a design for goods or manner of procedure or a creative idea invented by that individual or group for a specified time.

1.1 Classification of patents

According to stipulations of patent laws in many countries, the objects of patent protection are of the following three kinds：

＊ Invention or Creation(发明)：a new technical solution to a product, a method or to the improvement of the product or the method.

＊ Utility Model(实用新型)：a new technical solution applicable to the shape, the structure, or both of a product.

＊ Design or Mask(外观设计)：a new design of the shape, the structure, or both, of a product, which gives aesthetic feeling and has industrial applications.

1.2 Standard application

In general, patent application is in a format as follows (not necessarily with the following subtitles)：

＊ Title of the Invention；

* Field of the Invention (Technical Field) 技术领域：technical field that the to-be-protected invention belongs to；

* Background of the Invention (Background Art) 背景技术：related technical background or documents which contribute to the understanding, retrieval and examination；

* Summary of the Invention 发明内容：illustrate the problem to be solved by the invention or utility model and solutions adopted as well as their advantage effects（有益效果）compared with the prior art（现有技术）；

* Brief Description of the Drawings (Figures) 附图说明：brief illustration of drawings/figures；

* Detailed Description of the Invention (Embodiments) 具体实施方式：the preferred embodiment of the invention/utility model, with examples or drawings when necessary；

* What Is Claimed Is ... (Claims) 权利要求书/本专利权项范围；

* Assignment Form 转让形式；

* Cross Reference to Related Application（相关专利申请的交叉引用）.

1.3 Fixed format

The structure of a patent application is standardized, which usually consists of some regular items as mentioned above. Thus, patent application is a fixed-format document. For example：

ANTI-ICING SPRAY ASSEMBLY

BACKGROUND

The present invention relates to an anti-icing spray assembly and system, and in particular, to an anti-icing spray assembly that includes a watertight spray housing mounted in a base housing.

Various spray systems have been developed to apply anti-icing or anti-icing agents onto various roadways, including highways and airport runways. In some spray systems, as shown for example in U. S. Patent Nos. 6,102,306 and...

SUMMARY

Briefly stated, in one preferred embodiment described below an anti-icing spray assembly includes a base housing having a generally open top and a cavity. The base housing is adapted to be mounted in a roadway. A spray housing is removably secured to the base housing with at least a portion of the spray housing being disposed in the cavity of the base housing...

WHAT IS CLAIMED IS

1. An anti-icing spray assembly comprising：

A base housing having a generally open top and a cavity, wherein said base housing is adapted to be mounted in a roadway；a spray housing removably secured to said base housing with at least a portion of said spray housing being disposed in said cavity of said base housing, said spray housing defining an interior chamber, wherein said spray housing is watertight so as to substantially prevent water from entering said interior chamber, and herein said spray housing comprises at least one spray outlet adapted to spray an anti-icing agent onto the roadway；...

1.4 Structure of claims

Claim is the core part of patent application, including independent claim（独立权利要求）, and dependent claim（从属权利要求）.

1）Independent claim

It gives a general introduction of the technical solution of the invention or utility model and their characteristics, including preamble（序言）, a transitional word（过渡词）and a body（主体）.

＊Preamble：to describe the type of invention, which can be "an apparatus"（装置/设备）, "a method"（方法）, "a unit"（装置/构件）, "a composition"（组合物）, "a component"（组分）.

＊Transitional word：used after the preamble to introduce the parts, process or component of the technical solution, such as "comprising"（包括、包含）, "consisting of"（由……组成）, "consisting essentially of"（主要由……组成）, "characterized in that/characterized by"（其特点在于……）, wherein（其中）, provided that（假如）……, provided with（具有）.

Note：difference between "consisting of" and "comprising"：

consisting of A and B：只包括 A 及 B,无其他。

comprising A and B：除包括 A 及 B 外,还可能包括 C、D 等。

＊Body：the main part of claims, which differs according to different kinds of inventions. For example, for mechanical or electronic products, it should list all parts of the product in a logical order; in chemical field, chemical equation or molecular formula（化学方程式或分子式）should be included; as for methods, the description of steps to be followed are necessary.

Analysis：In the above sample

An anti-icing spray assembly comprising：

a base housing having a generally open top and a cavity, wherein said base housing is adapted to be mounted in a roadway...

Here "An anti-icing spray assembly" is the preamble, "comprising" the transitional word; the rest is the body part.

2）Dependent claim

It gives additional technical features and further limitations to independent claims. The frequently-used patterns are as follows：

（The method/name of apparatus）of claim 1...

（The method/name of apparatus）according to claim 1...

（The method/name of apparatus）as claimed in claim 1...

（The method/name of apparatus）as recited in claim 1...

（The method/name of apparatus）as defined in claim 1...

（The method/name of apparatus）as set forth in claim 1...

（The method/name of apparatus）in accordance with claim 1...

The above structures can be translated into "根据/如权利 1 所述……"

1.5　Linguistic features of patents

1）Uniform structure and expression

Similar structure and expression are often used in patent applications. For example：American patent consists of 6 parts：Cross Reference to Related Application, Technical Field, Background Art, Summary, Brief Description of the Drawings, Detailed Description. While Chinese patents basically include similar parts, "权利要求书, 技术领域, 背景技术, 发明内容, 附图说明, 具体实施方案" which can be readily translated into the equivalent in English.

2）Formal and precise diction

Both foreign and Chinese patent laws share similar requirements on the words and expressions used in patent application, namely, fullness, clearness, conciseness, exactness and professionalism. Patent applications have both the feature of EST and law, so it may have the most formal style. According to linguist Martin Joo's "Five Clocks" classification, there are five different English styles: frozen（庄重）, formal（正式）, consultative（商议）, casual（随便）and intimate（亲密）. Patent application is of frozen style with very precise diction.

For example, it uses "stoichiometry" to express 化学计量法 instead of "chemical metrology"; "interstice" but not "gap" for 间隙; "circumferentially" not "around" for 围绕; "embodiment" not "implementary scheme" for 实施方案; "a plurality of" not "a lot of/many/much/a large number" for 许多; "disclose（v.）/disclosure/publication" not "reveal" for（专利）公开; "adjacent or adjoin（ing）" not "neighbouring, close to or near" for 邻近、靠近; "resilient" not "flexible or elastic" for 弹性的（金属）; "elongated" not "long-shaped" for（长形）; "couple（vt.）" not "cooperate with, coordinate, combine, integrate" for 合作.

3) Use of archaic English and compound words

Since patent application is also a type of legal document, it still uses some legal terms, such as "pursuant to（按照）" "recite（书面陈述）" "ad hoc（特别）", and synonymous polymer（同义聚合词块）—combination of synonyms or parasynonyms（近义词）, such as "changes and alterations" "various and numerous"; and mediaeval words（中古词）like "said, here/there/where + prep.", etc.（see detail in next unit of contract）

4) More long sentences and loose structures

Section of "claims" often uses long sentences（100 – 500 words, see samples of the above "fixed format"）to list all the features or parts of the invention, and loose structure to put the most important information at the beginning of the sentence in order to insert more modifiers and clauses.

1.6 Translation of patents

1) Basic principle—faithfulness and smoothness

It means faithfulness to the original idea and style on one hand, and smooth expression on the other hand to be readily understood by the target readers.

2）Translation method—loan translation（套译）

As mentioned above, the structure of patent applications is similar, so are their typical sentence patterns. Therefore, it is quite necessary to copy the pattern in translation practice. Some fixed patterns are as follows：

（1）A(n) main/another/further object of the present invention is to (do)... OR It is a(n) main/another/further object of the present invention to (do)...

　　本发明的一个主要目的/另一个目的/再一个目的是……

（2）The present invention provides a (name of a/an apparatus/method/process), consisting of /comprising.../including..., wherein...

　　本发明提供了一种（装置/方法/工艺的名称），由……构成/包括……，其中……

（3）An apparatus for drying a liquid material comprising...

　　一种干燥液体材料的设备（装置），其包括……

（4）A polyethylene article having a surface treated in accordance with the process of Claim 3...

　　一种聚乙烯物品，具有如权利要求 3 所述的方法所处理的表面……

（5）A (name of a(n) apparatus/method/process), consisting of (comprising).../including..., characterized in that...

　　一种（装置/方法/工艺名称），由……构成/包括……，其特征在于……

（6）A process for preparing a compound of the following general formula：R-X, where in R is C1-C18 alkyl; and X is F, Cl, Br or I comprising...

　　一种制造下列通式化合物的方法：R-X，其中 R 为 C1-C18 烷基，X 为 F、Cl、Br 或 I，该方法包括……

（7）A (name of a(n) apparatus/method/process) as defined in/as recited in/in accordance with claim X, wherein...

　　如权利要求 X（数字）所述的（装置/方法/工艺名称），其中……

（8）This/The present invention relates to /is related to an apparatus /a method/a process...

　　本发明有关（关于/涉及）一种……的装置/方法/工艺……

（9）XX Patent No. xxxxxxx discloses a(n) apparatus/method/process (for)...

　　（某国）专利 xxxxxxx 号公开（披露）了一种设备/方法/工艺……

（10）The utility model is realized by the following technical scheme...

本实用新型通过下述技术方案予以实现……

（11）According to the first/second/third aspect of the invention, there provides an apparatus...

根据本发明的第一/第二/第三方面，提供一种装置……

（12）The foregoing descriptions of the embodiments and their accompanying drawings of the invention are intended to illustrate and not to limit this invention.

附图及上述介绍本发明的实例只是解释本发明，不是用来限制本发明。

（13）Reference is made to our co-pending application No. 345678 filed 13 May, 2013.

请参阅我们在 2013 年 5 月 13 日登记的与此有关的申请书，其申请号为 345678。

（14）This application is based on and claims priority of Patent Application Nos. 2012－233076 and 2014－145696, filed October 12, 2012 and July 23, 2014, respectively.

本申请基于分别于 2012 年 10 月 12 日和 2014 年 7 月 23 日提交的专利申请 No. 2012－233076 和 No. 2014－145696，并主张其优先权。

（15）We,（name of company and other information）, do hereby declare the invention, for which we pray that a patent may be granted to us, and the method by which it is to be performed, to be particularly described in and by the following statement...

我们（XX 公司）郑重公布本发明及实施本发明的方法。恳请贵专利局授予我们专利权。有关发明的细节详见下文……

1.7 Commonly-used terminology

1）Kinds of invention/patents

Invention patent(发明专利)；utility model patent（实用新型专利）；design patent（外观设计）专利；pending patent（未决专利：正在申请中的专利）；the disclosure（本发明）；continuation-in-part（接续专利）；letters patent（专利，专利证）.

2）Terms involved

Make reference to（参考,提及）；co-pending（与此有关的,尚待批准的）；royalty

（专利使用费）；Appl. No.（申请号）；Int. Cl. 3（International Patent Classification, 3rd Edition）国际专利分类表（第三版）；Ser. No.（流水号，档案号，申请号，登记号）；exemplary embodiments（示例性实施例）；apparatus/arrangement（装置）；device（器件）；means/member/element（构件）；preferably（最好，最佳选择）；Claims/We claim/What is claimed is/What we claim is（权利要求书）；prior art（现有技术/专利，先有专利，在先专利/技术）；those skilled in the art（所属领域技术人员）.

3）Kinds of figures

Accompanying drawings（附图）；preferred/alternative embodiments（最佳/另一个实施方案）；cross-sheet 5（第 5 页，图共 5 页）；sheet 3 of 4（第 3 页，图共 4 页）；view（视图）；FIG 1（图 1）；front/side/left/right/top（overhead, aerial）/bottom/rear view（正视图/侧视图/左/右视图/俯视图/底视图/后视图）；sectional/perspective/schematic/structural/exploded view（截面图/透视图/示意图（原理图）/结构图/爆炸图（分解图、立体图）；block diagram（方框图）；wiring diagram（线路图）.

Translation Practice 1

Translate the following into Chinese/English.

1. In the late 1800s, the Bell Telephone Company (established in 1877 by Alexander Graham Bell and his financial backers) used its patents to exclude others from the telephone business. After these patents expired, independent telephone companies emerged, but most of these were consolidated during the early 1900s by the American Telephone and Telegraph Company (AT&T), which had bought the Bell Telephone Company in 1900. In addition to owning virtually all of the long-distance circuits in the United States, AT&T manufactured most of the equipment, thus dominating all facets of the business.

AT&T was considered to be a "natural monopoly", and by law was decreed the sole provider of telephone service within a designated area. This arrangement reduced the costs associated with more than one company stringing wires in an area, and eliminated problems that had arisen when customers of one company wished to call customers of another company. In exchange for the absence of competition, these companies were regulated by government, which told them what services they must provide and what prices they could charge.

2. "Patented Technology" means such letters patent, and such applications for the patent as are presently owned or will hereafter be acquired in the future by Party B, or as Party B has or may have the right to control, or as are permitted to be transferred during the effective period of this Contract in any or all countries of the world, and as are applicable to or may be used in the manufacture of Contract Products specified by the Parties hereto.

3. Whereas Party B has the right and agrees to grant Party A the rights to use, manufacture and sell the Contract Products of Patented Technology; whereas Party A desires to use the Patented Technology of Party B to manufacture and sell the Contract Products; the Representatives authorized by the Parties to this Contract have, through friendly negotiation, agreed to enter into this Contract under the terms, conditions and provisions specified as follows...

4. 鉴于甲方拥有合同产品的生产和销售所涉及的技术信息，包括设计、技术、工艺、配方、技能和其他资料的专有权；鉴于乙方以生产、使用和销售合同产品为目的，希望获得使用上述协助的许可权利；鉴于乙方希望使用甲方所有的下述商标；双方兹就下列内容达成一致……

2. Copyrights

Copyright refers to a body of exclusive rights that protect the works of authors, artists, computer programmers, and other creative people against copying or unauthorized public performance. In other words, copyright is the body of legal rights that protect creative works from being reproduced, performed, displayed or disseminated by others without permission.

2.1 Classification of copyrights

Copyright is a legal protection extended to those who produce creative works. The following are specifically included:

(1) Literary works: novels, poems, and all works that do not fall into any other category.

(2) Musical works: original compositions and arrangements, and any accompanying works, including new versions of earlier musical compositions.

(3) Dramatic works: plays intended for live performance, and screenplays. The copyright covers music for dramatic productions, such as operas, musical comedies, and musi-

cal plays for television.

2.2 Terminology and institutions concerned with copyrights

(1) The Universal Copyright Convention (UCC) 万国版权公约

(2) The Copyright Clearance Center 版权批准中心

(3) Transfer of copyright 转让版权

(4) Copyright infringement 侵犯版权

2.3 Translation of copyrights

As a form of documentary style (公文文体), copyrights have their own characteristics that are different from other forms of written language. Therefore, in the translation of copyrights, due attention should be paid to the following points.

* Formal style. As a kind of official document, the language of copyrights is usually very formal and sometimes seems rigorous. When translated into Chinese, the original diction, style and form should be kept.

* Matter-of-fact-attitude. As a kind of objective description, works on copyright usually refrain from using pronouns. Instead, specific names for persons or things are given to particular matters. And some key words and expressions are frequently repeated to avoid ambiguity.

* Rigid grammar and frequent use of the passive voice. As a rule, works on copyright keep to a very strict English grammar. The passive voice is frequently adopted to meet the demand for objectivity.

Sample

RIGHTS ADDENDUM

This Addendum to the Translation/Adaptation and Co-Publishing Agreement entered into as of _____ between Thomson Learning, a division of Thomson Asia Pte Ltd. (hereinafter called TL) and (hereinafter called NOS) in conjunction with _____ As described in Section 2.2 of the above mentioned Agreement, NOS and WAP may proceed with the "Bilingual Edition" of the following "Work", subject to all conditions put forth in the Agreement and the attached Publication Proposal. This Addendum covers this "Work" in this edition and copyright year only. Any new version, edition, update or revision to the original "Work" and consideration for "Bilingual Edition" under the Agreement is not implied or guaranteed in this Addendum or Agreement and shall be subject to the signing of a new Rights Addendum.

Author: Jon Wright

Title: Idioms Organiser (Organised by metaphor, Topic and Key word)

Edition: 1st ed.

ISBN: 1 – 899396 – 06 – 3

Copyright Notice: 1999 by Henile & Heinle, a division of Thomson Learning

Initial Print Run: 10,000 copies

Authorized Edition: Bilingual Edition (Simplified Chinese/English)

New Oriental School　　Thomson Learning

SIGNATURE/DATE　　SIGNATURE/DATE

Translation Practice 2

Put the following passages into Chinese/English.

1. Copyright, body of legal rights that protect creative works from being reproduced, performed, displayed, or disseminated by others without permission. The owner of copyright has the exclusive right to reproduce a protected work; to prepare other works based on the protected work; to sell, rent, or lend copies of the protected work to the public; to perform protected works in public; and to display copyrighted works publicly. These basic exclusive rights of copyright owners are subject to exceptions depending on the type of work and the type of use made by others.

The term "work" used in copyright law refers to any original creation of authorship fixed in a tangible medium. Thus, works that can be protected by copyright include literary pieces, musical compositions, dramatic selections, dances, photographs, drawings, paintings, sculptures, diagrams, advertisements, maps, motion pictures, radio and television programs, sound recordings, and computer software programs.

Copyright does not protect an idea or a concept; it only protects the way in which an author has expressed an idea or a concept. If, for example, a scientist publishes an article explaining a new process for making a medicine, the copyright prevents others from copying the article, but it does not prevent anyone from using the process described to prepare the medicine. In order to protect the process, the scientist must obtain a patent.

2. 版权是一种无形资产。它所拥有的是一种权利。这种权利包括两个方面，即复制权和对复制权的使用控制。版权是对作品创造者实行的一种法律保护。最初仅限于对书籍方面，而今已扩大到对各种杂志、报纸、地图、戏剧、电影、电视节目、电脑软件、绘画、图片、雕塑、音乐作品及舞蹈动作设计等类作品的保护。实质上，版权保护的是知识或艺术财产。版权这种财产与众不同，因为它旨在为公众所利用，为公众所享受。

Unit 13   Scientific Literature（2）
Contracts and Agreements

Contract is any agreement between two or more parties that a court will recognize as creating legally binding duties and obligations between them.

1. Structure of Contract and Agreement

A contract or an agreement is usually composed of three main sections: preamble（约首）, body/text（正文）and witness clauses/final clauses/concluding clauses（约尾）. The preamble usually includes the names and statutory address of the parties concerned, the objectives and principles, *etc*. As the core of a contract, the text usually specifies the concrete rights and obligations of the parties concerned and other essential points. The concluding clauses are usually placed after the text.

The body part includes but not all of the following sections:
* Definition Clause 定义条款
* Basic Clause 基本条款
* General Terms and Conditions 一般条款
* Duration of Contract 合同有效期限
* Termination of Contract 合同的终止
* Force Majeure 不可抗力
* Assignment of Contract 合同的让与
* Arbitration 仲裁
* Governing Law 适用的法津
* Jurisdiction 诉讼管辖

＊ Notice 通知手续

＊ Amendment of Contract 合同的修改

＊ Others 其他条款

2. Linguistic Features of Contract

（1）The language is as precise, clear and explicit as possible.

（2）Use of such archaic words as "pacta sunt servanda（条约必须被遵守原则）" "ipso facto（依事实本身）""pursuant to（依照）".

（3）Frequent use of "shall", which means "a command or what must be done" or "the responsibility and obligation that should be undertaken" in the legal document. It is often translated into "应该、必须、一定". For instance：

Neither party shall terminate this contract without reasonable cause prior to the agreed date of expiration. 双方均不得无故提前终止合同。

（4）Use of such archaic compound words as "there/here/where + prep. ".

＊ here ＝ this

hereafter ＝ after this time（此后）

hereby ＝ by doing or saying so ＝ by means/reason of this（特此，兹）

herein ＝ in this piece of writing ＝ in this（此中，于此）

hereinafter ＝ after this time ＝ later in this paper（以下，在下文）

hereof ＝ of or belonging to this（在本文件中）

hereto ＝ to this piece of writing（本文件，至此）

heretofore ＝ until now, hitherto（迄今为止，在此之前）

hereunder ＝ below, following（在下文中）

hereupon ＝ at or after the time ＝ after that（因此，于是，随即）

herewith ＝ with this（与此一道，随函附上）

＊ there ＝ that

thereafter ＝ afterwards（此后，之后，其后）

thereby ＝ by saying or doing that ＝ by that means（因此，由此，在那方面）

therefor ＝ for that（因之，为此）

therefrom ＝ from that（从中）

therein ＝ in that piece of writing ＝ from that（在那里，在那点上，在其中）

thereinafter = later in the same paper（在下文中，以下）

thereof = of that（其中，由此）

thereon = on that（在其上，就此）

thereto = to that（××中的，随函附上）

thereunder = under that（在其下，依照）

thereupon = about that matter（关于此事）

therewith = with that（与此，与之）

* where = what/which

whereas = but（鉴于，但是）

whereat = at which（在哪儿）

whereby = by means of which = by what；by which（凭此协议；以……方式）

wherein = in which = in what（在其中，在那方面）

whereof = of which（关于）

whereto = to which（对于那个）

For example：

(1) All disputes arising from the performance of this Contract shall, through amicable negotiations, be settled by the Parties **hereto**.

对于因履行本合同所发生的一切争议，本合同双方应友好协商解决。

(2) The contractor shall not, without the prior consent of the Employer, assign the Contract or any part **thereof**, or any benefit or interest **therein** or **thereunder**.

没有业主的事先同意，承包人不得将合同或合同的任何部分，或合同中或合同名下的任何利益或好处进行转让。

(3) "Contract Products" mean the products specified in Appendix 2 to this Contract, together with all improvements and modifications **thereof** or developments with respect **thereto**.

"合同产品"，系指本合同附件 2 中规定的产品及其改进、发展的产品。

(4) This Law is **hereby** formulated and prepared in order to develop the foreign trade and maintain the foreign trade order. Foreign trade mentioned **herein** shall cover the import and export of goods, technology and the international trade in services.

为了发展对外贸易，维护对外贸易秩序，兹制定本法。本法所称对外贸易，是指货物进出口、技术进出口和国际服务贸易。

(5) The Leasee shall, at his own expense, keep the commodity in good condition. Provided that the Leasor shall be responsible for the breakdown of the commodity and the Leasee may have the right to lodge claims against the Leasor for any losses occurred **therein**.

承租人必须自负费用维持商品的良好状况;除非由出租人对商品的故障负责,承租人则有权向出租人提出赔偿因之所遭受的损失。

(6) **Whereas** Party A and Party B, adhering to the principle of equality and mutual benefit and through friendly consultation, agree to jointly invest to establish a new joint venture company in China (**hereinafter** referred as "Joint Venture"). The Contract **hereunder** is made and concluded.

鉴于甲方与乙方按照平等互利的原则，经过友好协商，决定在中国共同投资建立合资经营公司（以下称"合资企业"），为此达成如下合同。

5) **Use of coordinated structures**

by and between 由

complaints and claims 投诉及索赔

covenants and agreements 契约

customs fees and duties 关税

final and conclusive 最终及具决定性的

for and in consideration of 考虑到，鉴于

for and on behalf of 为了，代表

force and effect 效力

fulfill or perform 履行

furnish and provide 提供

goods and chattels 个人动产，有形动产

in full force and effect 生效

loss or damage 损失与损坏

make and enter into 达成

null and void 失效，无效

power and authority 权利

procure and ensure 保证和确保

release and discharge 弃权，让渡

right and interest 权益

save and except 除了

signed and delivered 签署并寄出

sole and exclusive 唯一且排他的

terms and conditions 条款

transferable or assignable 可转让的

under or in accordance with 按照(合同)

6) Use of double prepositions

(1) Our terms are cash within three months, i. e. **on and after** September 1.

我公司的条件是：3 个月内，即不得晚于 9 月 1 日，支付现金。

(2) Party A shall be unauthorized to accept any orders or to collect any account **on and after** October 12.

自 10 月 12 日起，甲方已无权接受任何定单或收据。

(3) The shipper shall be liable for all damage caused by such goods to the ship **and/or** cargo on board.

如果上述货物对船舶和(或)船上其他货物造成任何损害，托运人应负全责。

(4) This Contract is made **by and between** the buyer and the seller, whereby the buyer agrees to buy and the seller agrees to sell the under mentioned commodities subject to the terms and conditions stipulated below.

买卖双方同意按下述条款购买或出售下列商品并签订本合同。

7) Uniform sentence patterns

(1) This contract is made in two originals that should be held by each party.

此合同一式二份，双方各持一正本。

(2) What is left unmentioned in contract may be added there as an appendix.

本合同未尽事宜，可由双方增补作为合同附件。

(3) The Contract is written in quadruplicate (two for original and copy respectively) which shall become valid on the date of signature.

本合同一式四份（正副本各两份）自签署后生效。

(4) In the event of conflict between the provisions on arbitration formulated prior to the effective date of this Law and the provisions of this Law, the provisions hereof shall prevail.

本法施行前制定的有关仲裁的规定与本法规定相抵触的，以本法为准。

（5）This contract is executed in two counterparts each in Chinese and English, each of which shall be deemed equally authentic. This contract is in 2 copies effective since being signed/sealed by both parties.

本合同为中英文两种文本，两种文本具有同等效力。本合同一式两份，自双方签字（盖章）之日起生效。

（6）We hereby certify to the best of our knowledge that the foregoing statement is true and correct and all available information and data have been supplied herein, and that we agree to provide documentary proof upon your request.

特此证明，据我们所知，上述声明内容真实，正确无误，并提供了全部现有的资料和数据，我们同意，应贵方要求出具证明文件。

（7）This Contract is hereby made and concluded by and between XX Co. (hereinafter referred to as Party A) and XX Co. (hereinafter referred to as Party B) on XX (Date), in XX (Place), China, on the principle of equality and mutual benefit and through amicable consultation.

本合同双方，XX 公司（以下称甲方）与 XX 公司（以下称乙方），在平等互利的基础上，通过友好协商，于 XX 年 XX 月 XX 日在中国 XX（地点），特签订本合同。

8）Use of compounds and abbreviations

Compounds：full-enclosed（全封闭的）；feed-back（反馈）；work-harden（加工硬化）；on-and-off-the-road（路面越野两用的）；anti-armoured-fighting-vehicle-missile（反装甲车导弹）；radiophotography（无线电传真）；colorimeter（色度计）.

Abbreviations：lab（laboratory 实验室）；ft（foot/feet 英尺）；cpd（compound 化合物）；FM（frequency modulation 调频）；P. S. I.（pounds per square inch 磅/英寸）；SCR（silicon controlled rectifier 可控硅整流器）；TELESAT（telecommunications satellite 通信卫星）.

9）Use of nominalization（名词化结构）

It is to present a more concise, precise, and informative fact. For example：

（1）Archimedes first discovered the **principle of displacement of water by solid bodies**.

阿基米德最先发现固体排水的原则。

（2）**The rotation of the earth on its own axis** causes the change from day to night.

地球绕轴自转，引起昼夜的变化。

（3）Television is the **transmission and reception of images of moving objects by radio waves**.

电视通过无线电波发射和接受活动物体的图像。

10）**Use of passive voice**

According to John Swales from the University of Leeds（英国利兹大学）, about 1/3 of sentences are passive voice in EST.

For example, in EST, it is more proper to say "Attention must be paid to the working temperature of the machine" but not "You/We must pay attention to the working temperature of the machine." It can also be seen clearly from the above examples.

3. Translation of Contracts and Agreements

Similar to the translation of patent documents, the rendering of contracts and agreements also follows the principle of faithfulness and smoothness, conforming to the target convention. The method of loan translation is also applicable due to the similar sentence patterns and structures of these documents.

3.1 Sample translation of the preamble

This contract is made on this thirteenth day of September 2013 in Beijing by and between Beijing XX Co., Ltd. (hereinafter referred to as Party A) and Beijing XX Translation Company (hereinafter referred to as Party B).

Whereas exchanging of relevant business and technological information is required for the ongoing business discussions or cooperation between Party A and Party B with respect to the translation of technical data, this Contract is entered into by and between Party A and Party B through friendly consultations and under the principle of mutual benefit and joint development. The parties hereby agree as follows...

Chinese Version

本合同于 2013 年 9 月 13 日在北京签订。

合同一方为北京ＸＸ有限公司（以下简称甲方）；合同另一方为北京ＸＸ翻译

公司（以下简称乙方）。

鉴于甲乙双方正在就技术资料的翻译进行会谈或合作，需要取得对方的相关业务和技术资料，为此，甲乙双方本着互惠互利、共同发展的原则，经友好协商签订本合同。双方特定此协议如下……

3.2 Sample translation of the part of a text

1）Force Majeure

The Seller shall not be responsible for the delay of shipment or non-delivery of the goods due to Force Majeure, which might occur during the process of manufacturing or in the course of loading or transit. The Seller shall advise the Buyer immediately of the occurrence mentioned above and within _____ days thereafter the Seller shall send a notice by courier to the Buyer for their acceptance of a certificate of the accident issued by the local chamber of commerce under whose jurisdiction the accident occurs as evidence thereof. Under such circumstances the Seller, however, is still under the obligation to take all necessary measures to hasten the delivery of the goods. In case the accident lasts for more than _____ days the Buyer shall have the right to cancel the Contract.

2）Claim

The Buyer shall make a claim against the Seller (including replacement of the goods) by the further inspection certificate and all the expenses incurred therefrom shall be borne by the Seller. The claims mentioned above shall be regarded as being accepted if the Seller fails to reply within _____ days after the Seller received the Buyer's claim.

Chinese Version

1）不可抗力

凡在制造或装船运输过程中，因不可抗力致使卖方不能或推迟交货的，卖方不负责任。在发生上述情况时，卖方应立即通知买方，并在_____天内，给买方特快专递一份由当地民间商会签发的事故证明书。在此情况下，卖方仍有责任采取一切必要措施加快交货。如事故延续_____天以上，买方有权撤销合同。

2）索赔

买方凭其委托的检验机构出具的检验证明书向卖方提出索赔（包括换货），由此引起的全部费用应由卖方负担。若卖方收到上述索赔后 _____ 天未予答复，则认为卖方已接受买方索赔。

4. Terminology Concerning the Contracts and Agreements

Kinds of contracts：a long/short-term contract（长/短期合同）；contract for future delivery（期货合同）；contract for goods/purchase/service（订货/采购/劳务合同）；contract note（买卖合同/证书）；contract of arbitration（仲裁合同）；passenger/cargo carriage contract（客/货运合同）；technology development/transfer contract（技术开发/转让合同）；safekeeping contract（保管合同）；agency appointment contract（委托合同）；brokerage contract（居间合同）；multi-modal carriage contract（多式联运合同）；contract of employment（雇佣合同）；gift contract（赠与合同）；leasing contract（租赁合同）；contract of hired work（承揽合同）；executor contract（尚待执行的合同）.

Items of contract：the provisions of the Contract（合同条款）；any breach or default of the provisions hereof（任何违约及过失）；arbitration clause（仲裁条款）；contract amount incl. VAT & installation（合同总额,含安装费与税金）；payment conditions/terms（付款条件）；delivery place（交货地点）；delivery time（发货期）；installation clause（安装条款）；inspection clause（验收条款）；guarantee clause（保证条款）；breach clause（违约条款）；miscellaneous clause（其他条款）；cancellation of contract（撤销合同）；confidentiality obligations（保密义务）.

Frequently-used terms：including but not limited to（包括,但不限于）；transparency（图片）；specifications（规格）；assign（转让）；under the Contract（根据合同规定）；during the effective period of this Contract（本合同有效期间）；contract products（合同产品）；proprietary technical information（专有技术信息）；remark（备注）；contract life（合同有效期）；contract period/term（合同期限）；contract provisions/stipulations（合同规定）；contractual dispute（合同上的争议）；contractual liability/obligation（合同规定的义务）；contractual practice/usage（合同惯例）；contractual-joint-venture（合作经营,契约式联合经营）；copies of the contract（合同副本）；originals of the contract（合同正本）；execution of contract/performance of contract（履行合同）；expiration of contract（合同期满）；renewal of contract（合同的续订）.

Parties involved：Party A, Party B, a third party, the Leasee（承租人）；the Leasor（出租人）；the Buyer（买方）；the Seller（卖方）；contract parties（合同当事人）；the Contractor（订约人,承包人）；the Recipient Party（受让方），the Supplier（供方），the

Transferor（转让方）, the Transferee（受让方）, the Provider（提供方）, the Receiver（接受方）.

Translation Practice

1. Compare the following two texts and say: Which one is more formal Are they appropriately written in accordance with their respective occasion.

A. 北京 2008 年奥运会持票须知

①本须知是《北京 2008 年奥运会持票须知》的简略版本，您可在北京 2008 年奥运会官方票务网站 http://tickets. beijing2008. cn 上、场馆售票亭及《奥运会观众指南》上阅读完整版本。任何购买、持有或使用门票的人均被认为已经阅读、了解并接受了该完整版本。②北京奥组委有权在任何时候因任何原因宣布本门票无效。③ 门票不能被转售或交易。除非北京奥组委事先书面批准，门票不能被用于任何政治、宗教或商业目的。④开闭幕式门票仅能转让 1 次，且持票人仅能是购票人或经北京奥组委批准的受让人。⑤除非法律规定或北京奥组委明确告知，您不得申请退票或换票。如果某一场次在开始前被取消并不再另行安排，您可申请退票。如果您违反了持票须知完整版本里的任何一项，北京奥组委有权拒绝您入场或要求您离开场馆并不退换票。⑥您同意被北京奥组委、国际奥组委或他们指定的第三方拍照、摄影或录音等，并许可上述人员转播、出版，许可使用或使用您的上述记录，而不必给予任何补偿或因为该等使用而承担任何责任。⑦您用摄影机、录像机或声音设备或任何其他设备记录的北京 2008 年奥运会的图像和声音等只能用于私人的、非商业目的。⑧请不要携带任何中国法律明令禁止的物品入场，以及易碎品与各类容器；乐器；软硬包装饮料（医疗原因除外）及大量易投掷食品；球、球拍、飞碟及类似物品；大型箱包等；旗杆、非参赛国家或地区的旗帜，展开面积超过 2 米 × 1 米的旗帜；横幅和标语；未经授权的专业摄像设备和支架；动物（服务类动物除外）；除婴儿车与轮椅之外的任何代步工具；其他任何影响赛事顺利进行或防碍他人观赛的物品。⑨任何扰乱现场活动秩序和违反中国法律、法规的行为都是禁止的，包括但不限于集体使用或穿戴带有明显商业标志的包或服装或各类物品，未经授权的宣传展示活动和筹集资金的行为。⑩请按指定座位或区域就座。凭 1 张门票仅能进入场馆 1 次。⑪ 您须对您及跟随您的孩子的人身和财产安全负责。⑫您可凭当日门票（至次日凌晨 4 时）免费乘坐北京市域内公交车和地铁（不含郊区县公路客运、机

场快轨线）。您须自行核实交通信息并预留足够的安检时间。

English Version

Terms and Conditions of Sales and Use of Beijing 2008 Tickets

①This is a simplified version of the "Beijing 2008 - Terms and Conditions of Ticket Sales and Use". The complete version is available on the official ticketing website of the Beijing 2008 Olympic Games at http://tickets.beijing2008.cn, at all venue box offices and in the "Spectator Guide for the Olympic Games". Anyone who purchases, holds or uses a Ticket shall be deemed as having read, understood and accepted the complete Terms and Conditions. ② BOCOG has the right to invalidate any Ticket for any reason at anytime. ③ You cannot resell or trade your Ticket. You cannot use the Ticket for any political, religious or commercial purpose without the prior written approval of BOCOG. ④ Tickets to the Opening and Closing Ceremonies may only be transferred once and the Ticket holder must be the original purchaser or a transferee approved by BOCOG. ⑤You are not entitled to replace your Ticket nor receive refunds except as announced by BOCOG or where required by law. If a Session is cancelled before it is scheduled to start and is not re-scheduled, you may apply for a refund. In the event that you fail to comply with any of the complete Terms and Conditions, BOCOG shall have the right to refuse your entry, or request that you leave a Venue, without giving you a refund nor a substitution. ⑥ You consent to be photographed, filmed or taped by BOCOG, the IOC, the IPC or their authorized third parties, and any photographs, films, recordings or images of you may be broadcast, published, licensed and used without any compensation. The IOC, BOCOG, the third parties and anyone acquiring from them the right to use the material are not liable to you in any way for its use. ⑦ Images, videos and sound recordings of the Games taken by you with a camera, video camera or audio equipment or any other kind of equipment may not be used for any purpose other than private, non-commercial purposes. ⑧ Chinese laws and regulations prohibit you from carrying certain articles to the Venue. You should also not carry restricted articles to the Venue, such as breakable articles, containers, musical instruments, beverages (whether in soft or hard containers, except for medical reasons) and large quantity of easily-thrown food, balls, rackets, frisbees and similar objects, large objects such as suitcases, bags, flag poles, flags of countries or regions not participating in the Games, flags larger than 2 meters × 1 meter in size, signs, banners, unauthorized professional photography equipment, animals (except for those that provide services), transportation vehicles, devices or equipment（other than strollers and wheelchairs）, and any other articles that may affect the smooth and orderly progress of the Session or disturb other spectators attending such Session. ⑨ Any behavior that will disturb the smooth and orderly progress of the Games or violate Chinese laws and regulations is forbidden, such as unauthorized money collection, unauthorized promotional activity or display, and coordinating group use or wear of branded bags, clothing or anything with obvious commercial marks or symbols. ⑩ Please sit at your designated seat or areas. The Ticket is only good for one admission into a Venue. ⑪ You shall be responsible for the safety and property of both yourself and any children accompanying you. ⑫ You may use your Ticket to travel for free on the date marked on your Ticket（until 4 a. m. the next morning）by public bus and subway within the Beijing Municipality（excluding passenger transport to suburban districts and counties, and the airport express）. You are responsible for checking transportation information and setting aside enough time for security inspections.

B. 奥林匹克森林公园参观券持票须知

①本门票为奥林匹克公园外景参观凭证，持票人不得进入各竞赛场馆和非竞赛场馆。②持票人仅能根据票面指示时间进入奥林匹克公园指定区域参观，并在本门票所示参观时间终止前离开奥林匹克公园。③持票人在安检时应主动出示本门票，并服从安检要求。④本门票系免费提供，不能被交易或转让，如果丢失，应向发放单位报告。除非北京奥组委事先书面批准，门票不能被用于任何政治、宗教或商业目的。⑤北京奥组委有权在任何时候因任何原因宣布本门票无效。⑥持票人同意被北京奥组委、国际奥组委或其指定的第三方拍照、摄影或录音等，并许可上述人员转播、出版，许可使用或使用持票人的上述记录，而不必给予任何补偿或因为该等使用而承担任何责任。⑦持票人用摄影机、录像机或声音设备或任何其他设备记录的北京奥运会及残奥会的图像和声音等只能用于私人的、非商业目的。……⑨任何扰乱现场活动秩序和违反中国法律法规的行为都是禁止的，包括但不限于集体使用或穿戴带有明显商业标志的包或服装或各类物品，未经授权的宣传展示活动和筹集资金的行为。⑩持票人须对自身及孩子的人身和财产安全负责。⑪如果持票人违反了本持票须知规定，或在奥林匹克公园内从事了任何组织者认为不当的行为，组织者有权要求并采取措施使持票人离开奥林匹克公园。

English Version

Olympic Green Forest Park Visiting Ticket
Terms and Conditions of Sales and Use of Beijing 2008
Olympic Green Ticket

①This ticket is a ticket for visiting the outlook of the Olympic Green, and the holder can't enter into any competition venue or non-competition venue. ②Only with this ticket, the holder can enter into the designated area in the Olympic Green during the designated time, provided he leave the Olympic Green before the deadline marked on this ticket. ③The holder should show this ticket actively and follow the instructions when passing the security inspections. ④This ticket is offered for free and it cannot be resold or traded. The holder should report to the entity issuing the ticket if it's lost. The ticket can't be used for any political, religious or commercial purpose without the prior written approval of BOCOG. ⑤BOCOG has the right to invalidate this ticket for any reason at anytime. ⑥The holder consents to be photographed, filmed or taped by BOCOG, the IOC, the IPC or their author-ized third parties, and any photographs, films, recordings or images of the holder may be broadcast, published, licensed and used without any compensation. The IOC, BOCOG, the third parties and anyone acquiring from them the right to use the material are not liable to the holder in any way for its use. ⑦Images, videos and sound recordings of the Games taken by the holder with a camera, video camera or audio equipment or any other kind of equipment may not be used for any purpose other than private, non-commercial purposes ... ⑨Any behavior that will disrupt the smooth and orderly progress of the Games and Para-lymic Games or violate Chinese laws and regulations is forbidden, such as unauthorized money collection, unauthorized promotional activity or display, and coordinating group use or wear of branded bags, clothing or anything with obvious commercial marks or symbols. ⑩The holder shall be responsible for the safety and property of both himself and any chil-dren accompanying the holder. ⑪If the holder breaches these terms and conditions or enga-ges in any activities that the organizer deems inappropriate, the organizer has the rights to ask and take measures to make the holder to leave the Olympic Green.

2. Translate the following into English/Chinese.

(1) The Employer shall, prior to the submission by the Contractor of the Tender, have

made available to the Contractor, such data on hydrological and subsurface conditions as have been obtained by the Employer or the Representative on behalf of the Employer from the investigations into the Works provided that the Contractor shall be responsible for his own interpretation thereof.

(2) Modification and termination of a contract. Both parties shall abide by the contract. Neither party shall terminate this contract without reasonable cause prior to the agreed date of expiration. If Part A wants to terminate the contract before it expires, Party B shall be informed 30 days beforehand, and shall be given the reasons for breaking the contract during the term of service. If Part B wants to terminate the contract before it expires, he/she shall hand in a written request with the reasons for breaking the contract 30 days in advance. The contract becomes void automatically upon the expiration of the contract. Either party that makes a proposal for the extension of the contract shall put forward its request 4 days before the expiration of the contract. This contract is written in Chinese and English correspondingly, both texts being equally authentic.

(3) 如本协议因任何理由而终止，所有由甲方提供的图纸、图片、规格以及其他全部生产和操作资料，包括全部复制品，均返还甲方，同时，乙方应停止生产上述许可证产品、或部件、或零件。

(4) 承租人同意将所租房屋保持良好状态，并不得任其损坏。如果承租人对出租房屋作任何调整或增添任何设施，事先必须征得出租人的书面同意。房内任何增添和装修过的设施都成为出租人的财产，而且承租人不得以此向出租人提出补偿要求。如果发生火灾，本租赁合同立即终止。

Unit 14　Scientific Literature（3）
Proposals and Reports

1. Proposals

Proposal is a type of document written before work is performed to detail the work that needs to be done, typically written for audiences outside of your organization.

1.1 Classification of proposals

There are informal suggestions, semi-formal proposals and formal proposals.

1.2 Format for proposal

It usually includes the following parts:

（1）Statement of Need;

（2）Project Objectives;

（3）Statement of Procedures;

（4）Statement of Strength;

（5）Evaluation.

Sample of proposal

A Proposal to Research the Storage Facility for Spent Nuclear Fuel at
Yucca Mountain Roger Bloom

Introduction

Nuclear power plants produce more than 20 percent of the electricity used in the U-nited States [Murray,1989]. Unfortunately, nuclear fission, the process used to create this large amount energy, creates significant amounts of high level radioactive waste. More than 30,000 metric tons of nuclear wastes have arisen from U. S. commercial reactors as well as high level nuclear weapons waste, such as uranium and plutonium [Roush, 1995]. Because of the build-up of this waste, some power plants will be forced to shut down. To avoid losing an important source of energy, a safe and economical place to keep this waste is necessary. This document proposes a literature review of whether Yucca Mountain is a suitable site for a nuclear waste repository. The proposed review will discuss the economical and environmental aspects of a national storage facility. This proposal includes my methods for gathering information, a schedule for completing the review, and my qualifications.

Statement of Problem

On January 1, 1998, the Department of Energy (DOE) must accept spent nuclear fuel from commercial plants for permanent storage [Clark, 1997]. However, the DOE is undecided on where to put this high level radioactive waste. Yucca Mountain, located in Nevada, is a proposed site...

. . .

Another safety concern is the possibility of a volcanic eruption in Yucca Mountain...

Objectives

I propose to review the available literature about using Yucca Mountain as a possible repository for spent nuclear fuel. In this review I will achieve the following two goals:

(1) explain the criteria for a suitable repository of high-level radioactive waste; and

(2) determine whether Yucca Mountain meets these criteria.

. . .

Plan of Action

This section presents my plan for obtaining the objectives discussed in the previous section...

The first goal of my research is to explain the criteria for determining whether a nuclear waste repository is suitable...

A second goal of my literature review is to evaluate Yucca Mountain meets those criteria...

Management Plan

This section presents my schedule, costs, and qualifications for completing the proposed research. This research culminates in a formal report...

Conclusion

More than 30,000 metric tons of nuclear wastes have arisen from U. S. commercial reactors as well as high level nuclear weapons waste, such as uranium and plutonium [Roush, 1995]. This document has proposed research to evaluate the possibility of using Yucca Mountain as a possible repository for this spent nuclear fuel. The proposed research will achieve the following goals: (1) explain the criteria necessary to make a suitable high level radioactive waste repository, and (2) determine if Yucca Mountain meets these criteria. The research will include a formal presentation on November 11 and a formal report on December 5.

References

Kerr, R. , "New Way to Ask the Experts: Rating Radioactive Waste Risks," Science, vol. 274, (November1996), pp. 913 – 914.

. . .

1.3 Translation of proposals

Keep in mind the following points before starting the translation of a proposal.

(1) The purpose of the proposal — make sure it is a suggestion or a request, or an offer to solve a particular problem, or something else.

(2) The content of the proposal — try to be familiar with the content of the proposal: technical terms, specific means, measures and solutions.

(3) The relationship between or the identity of the proposal-writer and the receiver — this will guarantee the truthful representation of the original writing because it determines the final style of the proposal.

(4) The original tone and attitude — find out whether it is in a formal, semiformal or informal style and then reflect the original tone and attitude of the proposal in the translation.

Sample 1

Globalization of "Borders" Brand

Introduction

This proposal sets out to examine options for the successful globalization of our "Borders" brand. The initial market under consideration is Continental Europe. For the purposes of this proposal, we will be considering three aspects of the brand, namely our logo, the "Borders" concept and finally, the product itself, "Borders" Wellington boots.

Findings

The following points summarize our key findings.

● It was found that our existing logo, a pair of Wellington boots encircled by the word "Borders", is visual enough to be used in markets where English is not widely spoken.

● Attitudes to outerwear differ throughout Europe and our boots are likely to appeal to different market sectors in different countries. This has serious implications for the benefits we wish to publicise. Although Danish farmers would be willing to purchase such a high quality product, farmers in some countries would be unlikely to choose a British brand over a domestic product. However, the very Britishness of the product would appeal to the style-conscious elements of French and Italian markets, summoning up images of English upper classes and country houses.

● Our current product is multi-purpose and as such would not need adapting to suit different sectors of the European market.

Conclusion

It was agreed that although the present logo and product are suitable for globalization as they stand, we propose that the "Borders" concept be adapted for different markets.

Recommendations

We recommend that further studies be carried out into the marketing strategies best suited to different European regions.

Chinese Version

全球化的"边界"品牌

引言

本建议拟考察如何使我们的"边界"品牌获得全球化成功的几个方案。初步考虑的市场是欧洲大陆。之所以把该品牌定位于此，有三个方面的因素，即我们的标识，"边界"的理念和产品本身——"边界"惠灵顿靴子。

研究结果

以下几点总结了我们的主要研究结果：

● 我们发现，现有的标识——由"边界"（Borders）一词环绕的一双惠灵顿靴子，在没有广泛使用英语的市场视觉效果非常好。

●欧洲各国对待外衣的态度不同，在不同的国家我们的靴子可能会吸引到不同区域的市场。这就会严重影响我们希望达到的宣传效果。虽然丹麦的农民愿意购买这样的高品质产品，但一些国家的农民却很有可能不选择英国品牌，而选择国内产品。然而，典型英国特色的产品，很可能适合法国和意大利市场流行的风格元素，让人们想起英国上层阶级和乡村别墅的形象。

●我们目前的产品是多用途的，因此不需要适应欧洲市场，以满足不同行业的需要。

结论

大家一致认为，虽然目前的标识和产品宜于实现全球化，但我们建议的"边界"理念应该适用于不同的市场。

建议

我们建议进一步开展研究，找到最适合欧洲不同地区的营销策略。

Sample 2

新办公楼工程施工组织设计

首先，我们诚恳地表示：我们将全心全意为业主服务，服从业主、监理的管理，和设计单位、各方也单位一起共同完成本项目的建设任务。我们通过认真学习和研究招标文件及有关图纸资料，并踏勘施工现场，在分析了各种外部环境和内部条件以及工程施工的特点以后，我们有充分的信心保证高质量、如期、全面完成本工程招标文件规定的工程范围的任务。

一旦我们中标，我们一定会全力以赴，做好施工前期准备工作，并做好各项施工方案的审定工作。我们一定发挥我公司的管理、技术、队伍、材料、设备等资源优势，科学组织施工，配置足够的管理力量、技术力量和劳动力，强化计划管理、质量管理，在规定的合同工期内高质高速完成本工程，具体措施如下。

（1）把本项目列为我公司的重点项目，委派具有丰富现场管理经验和施工实践经验的项目经理担任项目部经理，配备施工经验丰富、技术素质高的管理人员组成项目管理班子，进驻现场施工。

（2）强化质量管理，严格按照建设部颁发的有关文明施工标准以及上海市建委关于施工现场标准化管理的具体规定组织好现场文明施工，确保达标，实现文明工地。

（3）工程施工采用信息化管理：施工过程中，按阶段采集施工信息，对施工操作过程进行摄像记录。项目施工的全过程采用计算机管理工程的工期、质量、技术、资源、文件档案。加强工程进度管理，提前规划，并在施工过程中采用先进的进度管理软件（Win Project）实行实时跟踪，及时调整作业计划，实现总体控制，确保在 215 个日历天完成所有施工任务。

（4）加强总承包管理措施，主动热情地组织好、配合好、协调好业主指定的其他分包单位施工，使本工程成为高品质的产品。

（5）以一流的服务、一流的干劲、一流的质量、一流的速度、一流的文明向业主献礼，为工程早日建成投入使用，早日发挥其社会效益和经济效益做出我们应有的贡献。

English Version

Construction Arrangement for New Office Building Project

First of all, we would sincerely state: we will serve whole-heartedly for the Client, subject ourselves to management by the Client and the Supervisor, and complete the project construction together with the design units and sub-contractors. After a careful study and research of the bidding documents and relevant drawings and documentations, we have made physical survey of the construction site, analyzed all kinds of external environment and internal conditions, and the characteristics of the project, and now we are fully confident that we can guarantee high-quality, timely and full completion of all the work stipulated in the tender documents.

We would go all out to do a good job in the pre-construction preparations and examination and approval of all the construction schemes if we won the bid. We are sure to play our advantages in management, technologies, teams, materials, equipment and other resources, to have scientific organization of construction, allocate sufficient personnel of management, technicians and the labor force, and to strengthen plan management, quality management so as to complete the project with high quality and speed within the specified contract period. The measures are as follows.

（1）We will take it as a key project of our company and assign a project manager with rich experience of site management and practical construction, and establish a site construction project management team composed of high-quality technical management personnel with rich experience in construction.

（2）We will strengthen the quality control and carry out the civilized construction in strict accordance with the relevant standards of civilized construction issued by Ministry of Construction and specific regulations of standardized site management by Shanghai Municipal Construction Committee so as to ensure the implementation of standards and realization of the civilized worksite.

（3）Information administration will be adopted during the project construction: In the course of project execution, we will collect all the information stage by stage and give video recording of the whole operation process. Computer program management will be applied in the whole process for the work period, quality, technology, resources and files. We will strengthen the project schedule management with everything planned ahead of time, and use advanced software（Win Project）to conduct real-time tracking, make timely adjustment of work plan, and implement an overall control so as to ensure the completion of all construction tasks within 215 calendar days.

（4）We will also reinforce the measures for the main Contractor management, and do a good and initiative job in organizing, cooperating, coordinating the work specified by the sub-contractors who are appointed by the Client so as to make the Project into a high-quality product.

（5）We will offer our Client first-class services, first-class quality and first-class civilization with our best efforts and speed, and make our due contribution to earlier completion and operation of the project in order to produce social and economic benefits.

Translation practice 1

Put the following passage into Chinese/English.

1. Throughout the world, devastating earthquakes occur with little or no advance warning. Some of these earthquakes kill hundreds of people. If the times, magnitudes, and locations of these earthquakes could be accurately predicted, many lives could be saved. This document proposes a review of how monitoring geophysical precursors can help in the short-term prediction of earthquakes. The proposed review will discuss the physical principles behind the monitoring of three common precursors and evaluate how accurate each monitoring is in predicting earthquakes. Included in this proposal are my methods for gathering information, a schedule for completing the review, and my qualifications.

I propose to review the available literature on how geophysical precursors can be used for short-term predictions of earthquakes. In this review, I will achieve the following three goals: 1) explain three commonly monitored geophysical precursors—ground uplift and tilt, increases in radon emissions, and changes in the electrical resistivity of rocks; 2) show what happens to each of these precursors during the five stages of an earthquake; and 3) discuss how each of these precursors is used for short-term earthquake predictions.

2. 一般来说，管理性建议向预期的客户准确地解释整个项目将如何进行管理，以及管理人员情况等，并为完成该项目提出一个时间进度表。管理性建议的重要目的之一是让客户相信，该项工作在每个阶段都将由能胜任的人员来完成，包括原型设计研究到整个制造阶段，初始的探索性研究到最终解决方案。此外，建议中有关管理的部分应当在质量和可靠性问题上分清职责，措辞要尽量清晰果断，便于客户与供应商有效交换意见。

2. Reports

Reports communicate a wide variety of information, mostly describing various aspects of work that has been or needs to be completed. Reports are written for both external audiences (clients or other personnel outside of your organization) and internal audiences (supervisors, managers, or other colleagues within your organization).

2.1 Classification of reports

We have informal reports, semiformal reports, and formal reports.

2.2 Linguistic features of reports

1) Various patterns

(1) Letter form report

(2) Schematic form report

(3) Short report (or Summary report)

2) More active voice

The pronoun "I" is readily evident in the informal memo reports.

3) Standard language

The language used is normally not complex but straightforward. It is brief yet fully informative.

2. 3 Translation of reports

It is similar to the translation of proposals. The following is a sample of Report and its Chinese version.

Wind Farms *vs*. Wildlife

The Shocking Environmental Cost of Renewable Energy

According to a new study, wind farms are devastating populations of rare birds and bats across the world, driving some to the point of extinction. Most environmentalists just don't want to know because they're so desperate to believe in renewable energy, and they're in a state of denial. But the evidence suggests that, in this century at least, renewables pose a far greater threat to wildlife than climate change.

I'm a lecturer in biology and human sciences at Oxford University. I dreamed to be a zoologist, but I've worked as an environmental consultant—conducting impact assessments on projects like the Folkestone-to-London rail link—and I now teach ecology and conservation. Though I was neutral on renewable energy initially, I've since seen the havoc wreaked on wildlife by wind power, hydro power, biofuels and tidal barrages. The environmentalists who support such projects also realize so for ideological reasons. What few of them have in their heads, though, is the consolation of science.

My specialty is species extinction. When I was a child, my father used to tell me about all the animals he'd seen growing up in Kent—the grass snakes, the lime hawk moths—and what shocked me when we went looking for them was how few there were left. Species extinction is a serious issue: around the world we're losing up to 40 a day. Yet environmentalists are urging us to adopt technologies that are hastening this process. Among the most destructive of these is wind power.

...

Why is the public not more aware of this carnage? First, because the wind industry has gone to great trouble to cover it up to the extent of burying the corpses of victims. Second, because the ongoing obsession with climate change means that many environmentalists are turning a blind eye to the ecological costs of renewable energy. What they clearly don't appreciate—for they know next to nothing about biology—is that most of the species are threatened by 'climate change' and sea-level rises far more dramatic than any we have experienced in recent millennia or expect in the next few centuries. Climate change won't drive those species to extinction; well-meaning environmentalists might. (Clive Hambler, A lecturer in the Department of Zoology, University of Oxford, UK. 5 January 2013)

Chinese Version

风电场：野生动物杀手
——可再生能源带来的巨大环境成本

一项最新研究表明，风电场正在使世界上大量的稀有鸟类和蝙蝠的数量锐减，甚至导致一些物种濒临灭绝。大多数的环保人士都不想面对这样的现实，因为他们盲目信任可再生能源，也不愿承认这样的事实。但是证据表明，至少在本世纪，与气候变化相比，可再生能源对野生动物造成的威胁要大得多。

我是牛津大学生物与人类科学专业的一名讲师。我曾经想成为一名动物学家，却当了一名环境顾问，对一些项目进行影响评估，如福克斯顿到伦敦的铁路项目。我现在教授生态学与自然资源保护这门课。尽管最初我对可再生能源持中立态度，但渐渐发现风能、水能、生物燃料和潮汐堰坝对野生动物造成了巨大破坏。一些支持这些项目的环保人士，也从思想上认识到这些问题的严重性。不过，这些人能想到的仅仅只是科学的慰藉而已。

我的专业是研究物种灭绝问题。很小的时候，父亲就常告诉我他见过的生活在肯特的所有动物，诸如草蛇、交鹰蛾。但令我震惊的是，我们去寻找这些动物的时候，才发现它们已经所剩无几。物种灭绝问题十分严峻：全球每天消失的物种超过40个。尽管如此，环保人士依然敦促我们采用一些技术加快物种灭绝的速度，而其中最具有破坏性的就是风能。

……

为什么这种残杀还没有引起人们的重视？第一，风力发电产业试图努力掩盖真相，毁尸灭迹。第二，许多环保人士密切关注气候变化，因此对可再生能源带来的生态代价视而不见。他们对生物学几乎一无所知，所以显然没有意识到多数物种会受到气候变化的威胁，而且海平面快速上升，这种速度是我们在近千年从未经历过的、在未来几百年也不会预料到的。气候变化并不会使这些物种灭绝，而怀有良好愿望的环境学家却有可能让它们灭绝。

Translation Practice 2

Put the following passage into Chinese/English.

1. The 2013 Clean Energy Australia Report shows how renewable energy and energy efficiency are helping to build a stronger, cleaner economy. From jobs and investment in regional areas to solar panels, solar hot water and high efficiency appliances right across the country, clean energy contributed billions of dollar's worth of economic activity during the 2013 calendar year.

Even better news is that Australia's Renewable Energy Target can actually lead to lower power prices in the long run...

This is because fewer renewables such as wind and solar would mean more of our energy would have to come from gas-fired electricity, which is getting more expensive all the time. The Australian Industry Group (AiGroup), which represents many of the country's large manufacturers and other energy users, said in 2014 that the rising price of gas is emerging as possibly the biggest energy issue we face. AiGroup and others have projected that gas prices may triple this decade, causing major bill shock for some of our more energy-intensive industries.

The Clean Energy Australia Report shows how the Renewable Energy Target has already achieved much; all it needs now is to be left alone to do the rest of its job. Key to this is a stable environment policy where investors can support clean energy projects with confidence that government won't move the goal posts. With the right policy settings for a stable investment environment, clean energy will help Australia's economy go from strength to strength.

2. 读书报告是学校布置的书面或口头作业,用于讨论和评价书的内容。写读书报告时,首先要给出书的题目、作者、出版社及出版年代。有时候简单总结一下书的内容有助于读者了解其大概。不过,读书报告中最重要的部分应该是你自己对书的评价意见。该书的读者对象是谁?作者要达到的目的是什么?与同类书的作者相比,该作者有多么成功?书的优、缺点是什么?在回答这些问题时,应该提供具体的理由支持自己的观点,包括从书中选取细节和引语。读书报告的结尾处要陈述自己对该书的总体意见。读书报告的讨论内容取决于所评论的书的类型。例如,有关小说的读书报告,应该包括故事情节、背景及人物方面的信息,还应该评价一下小说的总体影响或意义。

Unit 15　Scientific Literature（4）
Scientific Papers

1．Translation of Title

Title of a paper is often featured by nominalization with concise, precise, formal language. Compare the following two versions：

（1）科技翻译方法初探

    A：Preliminary Study of Methods of Scientific Translation

    B：Methods of Scientific Translation

（2）机器翻译系统可靠性探讨

    A：Discussion on Reliability of Machine Translation System

    B：Reliability of Machine Translation System

（3）自然资源与环境的研究

    A：Research on Natural Resources and Environment

    B：Natural Resources and Environment

（4）论建筑学与现代科学技术

    A：On Architecture and Modern Scientific Techniques

    B：Architecture and Modern Scientific Techniques

（5）论公关工作在全面质量管理中的作用

    A：Function of Public Relation Work in Total Quality Control

    B：Function of Public Relation in Total Quality Control

（6）关于建筑产品质量问题的法津思考

    A：A Consideration from the Angle of Law on the Problems in Quality of Building Products

B：A Consideration from the Angle of Law on the Quality of Building Products

（7）论劳动力市场需求约束条件下的经济模式

A：The Economic Model Restrained by the Condition in Market Demands of Labour Force

B：The Economic Model Restrained by Market Demands of Labour Force

2. Translation of Abstract

An abstract is a statement summarizing the important points of a text at the beginning of a document, such as a scientific paper. It is a concise and accurate representation of the contents of a document, in a style similar to that of the original document. It is a short description, or a condensation, of a piece of writing.

2.1 Classification of abstracts

There are two types of abstracts: descriptive and informative abstract.

1) Descriptive abstract

A descriptive abstract says what you do in the work without providing any information or results. It is a topical or table-of-content abstract, a more appropriate representation of discussion and review articles, books and conference proceedings, reports without conclusions, essays and bibliographies. They abound in sentence patterns such as "is discussed" or "has been investigated", yet do not record the outcome of the discussions or investigations.

2) Informative abstract

An informative abstract says what the work contains, including summarizing the main results. It is also called an executive summary, presenting as much as possible of the quantitative or qualitative information contained in a document, a clear condensation of essential arguments and findings of the original. It also answers the question, "What are the important points made in the writing?"

Sample of descriptive abstract

This report describes the advantages and disadvantages of each of the options available for dealing with the problem of increased air passenger traffic to Newtown and provides a recommendation for a way forward.

Sample of informative abstract

This report describes four options available for dealing with the problem of increased air passenger traffic to Newtown. The options are

Build a new runway at the existing airport

Build a new airport in Newtown West

Build a new airport 30 miles north

Do nothing

The first three options will all provide a short-term boost to the local employment market, while options 2 and 3 will provide long-term economic benefits. Option 1 is relatively cheap, but will only provide a short-term solution. Option 2 is expensive and unpopular with local Newtown residents. Option 3 is more popular, but just as expensive. However, there is a possibility of a higher government subsidy for option 3. Option 4 is likely to be ruled out after the result of the next local elections. We recommend option 3.

2.2 Linguistic features of abstract

1) Diction

Abstract is precise, concise and more formal in wording. Care must be exercised to avoid ambiguity, and redundant phrases such as "the authors studied" "in this work" "the paper concludes by", *etc.* should be avoided if possible.

2) Grammar

(1) Use the third persona, "the author" "the paper" is preferred to "I" or "we".

(2) Use simple past tense to indicate things done in the past or to describe the things the author has done.

(3) Use simple present (perfect) tense for the conclusion drawn from the work.

(4) Use future tense (be to do) for the aim/goal/purpose of the paper.

(5) Use more passive voice than active voice.

3) Sentence structure

(1) Use more indicative sentences, with verbs close to the subject.

(2) Use brief and informative sentences.

(3) Sentences with an average length at about 12 words are likely to yield a readable

abstract.

(4) Avoid the sentence beginning with a phrase or clause, more often starting with the important fact.

4）Arrangement

All abstracts, barring possibly those of exceptional length, should consist of one paragraph only. This should be a coherent paragraph, but not a series of disjointed sentences.

2.3 Formation and sentence pattern of an abstract

1）Topic sentence

（1）本文介绍/讨论/详细论述/提出……

This paper/article describes （introduces/discusses/elaborates/focuses on/raises/proposes）...

... is/are studied （discussed/shown/presented/introduced/proposed/analyzed/explained）in this paper/article

（2）作者提出/试图……

The author /writer presents/endeavors to ...

（3）本文的目的是解释/介绍/讨论……

The purpose/object of this article/contribution is to explain/describe/discuss /introduce...

（4）本文的主要目的有三……

This paper has three main objectives...

（5）该项科研项目致力于……

This research project is devoted to...

（6）本文提供了有关……的详细信息

Detailed information is presented about...

（7）本文对……作了研究。

A study has been made of ...

（8）本文（论文、报告等）论述（详细说明、调查、包含、涉及）了以下问题……

This paper（thesis, report, etc.）addresses（specifies, examines, covers, is concerned with etc.）the following questions...

（9）本文（文章、报告、论文、文献、著作、报道等）阐述（报告、说明、总括、讨论、概述、展开、调查、分析、评价）了……的结果（方法、作用）

This paper（article, report, thesis, document, work, account, etc.）describes（reports, explains, outlines, discusses, summarizes, develops, surveys, investigates, analyzes, etc.）the results（approaches, roles, etc.）of...

2）Supporting sentences

（1）实验/实例 显示/表明/证实……

Experiments/examples demonstrate/show/confirm...

（2）……被提出/验证/引自/分析……

...are/is given/verified/derived from/analyzed...

3）Concluding sentences

（1）结果（发现、数据、实例等）表明（显示出，提出等）……

Results（findings/examples）show（demonstrate/indicate/suggest）.../It shows.../The results...are given/presented...

（2）结论为……/我们的结论是……

This concludes that.../It is concluded that.../We conclude that...

（3）作者建议……

The author proposes.../...is proposed（by the author）.

（4）现已发现（观察、证实）……

It has been found（observed, shown/proved, etc.）that...

（5）这个方法证实对……很有用。

The approach（method, etc.）promises to be very useful for...

（6）希望本研究对未来的……有一定的指导意义。

It is hoped that the present study would be of some guidance to the future...

2.4 Problems in abstract translation

1）Using improper and wordy expressions

（1）本文提出了一种新的计算机辅助翻译方法。

A：A new computer-aided translation method is **put forward** in this paper.

B：A new computer-aided translation method is **presented**（in this paper）.

（2）本文为提高打印速度和印字质量提供了一种机辅设计手段。

A：This paper presents a CAD method for **increasing** the printing speed and the printing quality.

B：This paper presents a CAD method for **improving** the printing speed and the printing quality.

2）Using colloquial or informal style

（1）本文主要研究平面机构的可动性。

A：This paper **mainly** studies the movability of planar mecharvism.

B：This paper **principally** studies the movability of planar mecharvism.

（2）通信工程师对作者所讲的内容很感兴趣。

A：**The content that the author talks about** is of great interest to communications engineers.

B：**What this paper describes** is of great interest to communications engineers.

3）Inflexible translation by following the original order and expression

As we know, nominalization structures are often used in the form of phrases to express an action, so as to make it more concioc, definite, compact and objective.

（1）本文对该设备的性能进行了分析。

A：The performance of this device is analyzed（in the paper）.

B：An analysis of the performance of this device is made.

（2）简要介绍了磁悬浮列车的基础知识。

A：Fundamentals of a maglev are briefly introduced.

B：A brief introduction is given to the fundamentals of a maglev.

（3）本文对最近推荐的一种方案作了研究。

A：This paper studies a recently-recommended scheme.

B：A study has been made of a recently-recommended scheme.

4）Starting the sentence with numbers

（1）本论文分析了36个作文范本。

A：36 sample writings are analyzed in this paper.

B：Thirty-six sample writings are analyzed in this paper.

Or：This paper analyzes 36 sample writings.

5）Starting the sentence with a phrase or clause excluding important facts

（1）从实验数据可以确定反应堆余烬的燃料消耗量。

A：From data obtained experimentally, fuel consumption in a reactor core was determined.

B：Fuel consumption in a reactor core was determined from data obtained experimentally.

6）Verb far from the subject

（1）本文针对当前我国对外经济法规汉英翻译的一些实际问题，探讨了以翻译规律来规范对外经济法规汉英翻译的可能性。

A：This paper, aiming at some obvious errors in translating current China's foreign economic laws and rules, discusses the possibility of governing the C-E translation of those documents.

B：This paper discusses the possibility of governing the C-E translation of current China's foreign economic laws and rules after analyzing some obvious errors in translating.

7）Monotonous structure

（1）环流反应器在工业上正得到越来越广泛的应用，对其进行深入研究对于此类反应器的设计与放大具有重要意义。对环流反应器的流动、混合及传质特性参数随表观气速、液相物性、系统压力和反应器尺寸等操作条件的变化关系进行了综述。介绍了各特性参数的测量方法，并指出了这些方法的优缺点及可能存在的误差。对环流反应器的流动、混合及传质特性的数学模型进行了评述，并在此基础上对环流反应器研究的发展前景进行了展望。（何广湘等，化学工业与工程，2008，1）

Original Version

Airlift loop reactors（ALRs）have been **widely used** in industry, so the investigation of ALRs is very important for their design and scale-up. The effects of operating conditions, such as superficial gas velocity, liquid properties, system pressure, reactor size, on the behavior of ALRs **were discussed** and the measuring methods for the reactor behavior **were introduced**, also their deficiency **was pointed out**. The mathematical models of flow behavior, mixing and mass transfer in ALRs **were reviewed**.

Suggested Version

Airlift loop reactors（ALRs）have been widely used in industry, so the relevant investigation is very important for their design and scale-up. This paper discusses the effects of operating conditions, such as superficial gas velocity, liquid properties, system pressure, reactor size, on the behavior of ALRs. It also introduces the measuring methods for the reactor behavior and their deficiency as well. Eventually, the mathematical models of flow behavior, mixing and mass transfer in ALRs were reviewed.

2.5 Translation principles

（1）Be aware of the purpose of the abstract to be translated.

（2）Be familiar with the entire document whose abstract is to be translated.

（3）Be succinct in wording.

2.6 Ways of translating Chinese abstract

1）Breaking-up

（1）本文对去污工艺的化学、物理过程进行了理论分析，认为氧化去污机理是 6 种化学反应的联合进行，还提出了去污剂选择的理论依据。

This paper has analyzed theoretically the chemical and physical process of decontamination. The author holds that mechanism of oxidation decontamination consists in combination of six chemical reactions. The scientific bases for selecting decontaminants are proposed as well.

（2）机器翻译技术及各类翻译软件已在很大程度上改变了传统的人工翻译模式，降低了翻译的劳动强度，提高了翻译效率，如将其用作外文翻译的辅助工具，用途的确非常广泛，尤其科技翻译受益匪浅。但因受制于关键技术及涉及跨文化交流的内涵，机译及翻译软件无法区分文本的感情色彩，因而它们将注定不能取代人工翻译的主宰作用。

Machine translation technology and various translation softwares have dramatically changed the traditional human translation mode. They have reduced labor intensity in human translation and enhanced translation efficiency. Indeed, they can serve various purposes if used as auxiliary tools in translation of foreign languages, especially that of science and technology. However, machine translation and translation softwares are unable to differentiate sensational elements due to constraints on crux technology and implications of cross-cultural exchange. Hence, they cannot replace the dominant role of human translation.

2）Combination

（1）本文比较了 STM 和 ATM。结果表明 ATM 是 BISDN 的基础。

A comparison between STM and ATM shows that ATM will be the basis of BIS-DN.

（2）本文提出了解决这一问题的新方法。这种方法简单而又切实可行。

A new method for solving this problem is presented, which is simple and practicable.

（3）煤矿水灾害会对煤矿企业造成巨大的损失。选择有效的煤矿水灾害救治系统可以最大程度降低其损失。

Coal-mine flooding will bring great economic losses and casualties to coal enterprises, so an effective rescuing system can greatly reduces such losses.

Analysis

In terms of sentence structures, there are often two types of Chinese abstracts. One is featured by one or two long sentences with some fixed structures/patterns like "基于/针对……，阐述/分析……，剖析/论证……，提出/提供……. In this case, the translator should clearly analyze the logical relations among different elements, and divide them into different coherent sentences. The other is written with several short sentences and sometimes with subjects/conjunctions omitted, so the combination method is often adopted.

Sample 1

从信息论的角度**分析了**一个典型的两步量子直接通信方案的安全性，**计算了**该量子直接通信过程中攻击者 Eve 所能获得的信息量及在 Eve 进行攻击后合法通信者所能接收的信息量，为合法者对量子直接通信的安全性判定和对敌手的检测**提供了**一定的依据和标准。（周南润等，量子光学学报，2008，4）

Original Version

The security of a typical scheme of the two-step quantum direct determinant communication **is analyzed** from the aspect of information theory. **The amount of information which** the eavesdropper and the legal receiver can get **is calculated**, **which** can serve as a criteria for checking Eve and estimating the security of quantum direct communication between legal communicators.

Analysis

This is a quite typical Chinese abstract consisting of only one sentence with the fixed pattern but without obvious subject：分析了……计算了……提供了……

The above translation turns one Chinese sentence into two English passive sentences. And subjects are either chosen from the original or added to conform to English norms (see the italicized). The second sentence is a much longer containing one passive voice, one active voice and two "which", so the structure is a little complex for an abstract. It is better to divide it into two parts. What is more, the two sentences are mainly literally translated by following Chinese paratactic structure without clearly indicating the logical relations with some connectives. Besides, "criteria" is a plural form, here it should be a single form ("criterion").

Suggested Version

This paper first analyzes from the aspect of information theory the security of a typical scheme of the two-step quantum direct determinant communication. **Then the amount of information** that the eavesdropper and the legal receiver can get is calculated. **Therefore**, **the research** can serve as a **criterion** for checking Eve and estimating the security of quantum direct communication between legal communicators.

Sample 2

提出了一个利用一束单光子对话的方案。在方案中，利用两个不同的幺正操作对光子态进行编码，并且从一束光子中选择较大的子集进行窃听检查，该方案能够有效地抵御截取再发送袭击。此外，由于利用单光子没有利用 EPR 对，因此该方案是很实际的。该方案是绝对安全的。(计新等，量子光学学报，2008，3)

Original Version

We propose a quantum dialogue scheme using a batch of single photon. In the scheme, **we** encode the states of the single photons with the secret message by two different unitary operations, and select randomly a sufficiently large subset of photons from the batch to check eavesdropping, so **our scheme** can resist the intercept-and-resend attack efficiently. In addition, **our scheme** is practical because it uses single photons instead of EPR pairs. The conclusion shows that the scheme is unconditionally secure.

Analysis

This is another typical Chinese abstract with a few short sentences. It is written with a combination of Chinese and English structures, having subjects omitted in the first two sentences but many conjunctions "并且……,此外……,由于……,因此" used.

The above translation follows the original order and logical relation with some repeated addition of subjects (we..., we...our..., our..., the conclusion...) and more conjunctions (so, instead of) according to the implied logic. The problems are as follows：

First of all, the whole abstract lacks variety with all four sentences in active voice. And the second sentence is longer, wordy, illogical and ungrammatical. Besides, the connective "so" is used improperly in that context in both meaning and structure. Finally, EPR is better given a full name for facilitating reader's reading. And the style is informal.

Suggested Version

This paper proposes a quantum dialogue scheme using a batch of single photon. **The scheme** is to encode the states of the single photon with two different unitary operations, and check eavesdropping to a sufficiently large subset of photons from the batch. **It is proved** that our scheme can resist the intercept-and-resend attack efficiently. Additionally, **it** is practical and absolutely by using single photon instead of electron paramagnetic resonance (EPR) pairs. **It** is concluded that the scheme is Unconditional secure.

Translation Practice

Put the following passages into English.

1. 阐述了 2000 年以来中国经济和能源消费快速增长的态势以及能源消费的构成变化情况和石油消费形势，探讨了 2050 年前几种不同情景下的中国经济增长前景、能源消费增长趋势、能源消费构成变化趋势和石油需求总量。

2. 加快发展常规天然气、页岩气、煤层气等气体能源，既能有效缓解我国面临的能源安全、环境保护和减排等多重压力，又能培育新的经济增长点。为此，应提升气体能源在我国能源战略中的地位，加快能源领域的市场化改革，建立和完善准入和矿业权管理制度，放宽气体能源的行业准入，改革能源价格形成机制，并加大对页岩气开采等关键技术开发的支持，从而改变我国能源供应和消费的结构，支持可持续发展和生态文明建设。

Unit 16　Scientific Literature（5）
Conference Documents

Conference documents include all printed materials from the preparation of a conference to the post-conference proceedings.

1. Documents in the Preparation of a Conference or Symposium

Documents in the preparation of a conference or symposium consist of Announcements and Call for Papers or Participation; Instructions for Authors; Instructions for Speakers; Registration Form; Accommodation Registration Form; Invitations, and General Information containing preliminary Time Schedule, *etc*. For example:

2014 IEEE World Congress on Computational Intelligence

2014 年 IEEE 世界计算智能大会

Call for Papers

The IEEE World Congress on Computational Intelligence (IEEE WCCI) is the largest technical event in the field of computational intelligence. The 2014 International Joint Conference on Neural Networks (IJCNN 2014) is the flagship conference of the IEEE Computational Intelligence Society and the International Neural Network Society. It covers all topics in the field of neural networks from biological neural network modeling to artificial neural computation.

...

All papers should be submitted electronically through the Congress website. Contributed papers will be refereed by experts in the fields based on the criteria of originality, significance, quality and clarity.

2. Documents Distributed at a Conference or Symposium

Documents distributed at a conference usually include: conference program with all sessions, workshops, and other social activities listed; Book of Abstracts or Conference Proceedings (or Preprints volume) including Conference Paper Abstracts; Conference Daily Schedule, and so on. For example:

Welcome

Dear participants,

Welcome to Beijing & Hong Kong and to the 7th International Symposium on Applied Linguistics & Language Teaching (ISALLT)! This symposium is a joint initiative of Beihang University and The Hong Kong Polytechnic University with co-sponsorship by the University of Silesia, Poland. Applied linguistics and foreign language researchers and practitioners in the language teaching and research community from all over the world will convene together, to discuss their common interests, share their different experiences, exchange their ideas and innovations in applied linguistics and language teaching, and to see the rapidly developing China. Below is some general information about the 7th ISALLT, which we hope will be helpful to you.

3. Documents Distributed after a Conference or Symposium

Documents distributed after a conference usually include: post-conference proceedings. This may be the permanent record of the conference or symposium; some special issue of selected papers in a certain journal; newsletters for some regularly-held conferences, which are issued at regular intervals for the purpose of disseminating current information relevant to an academic organization, *etc.*

4. Translation Principles

Conference documents are of various types. So it is hard to generalize translation skills. However, the principles below should be followed.

● Acquire as much as possible knowledge of the specialty related to the document and try to be familiar with its professional terms and background of the translation materials.

● Have a global idea of the document to be translated and see to it that the original point of view is properly expressed in the Chinese/English version.

● Adopt formal language style and structure instead of colloquial ones.

The following is a sample of conference document and its Chinese version.

FIT XXth World Congress
Berlin, August 4 – 6, 2014
Call for Papers

FIT (International Federation of Translators) is an international grouping of associations of translators, interpreters and terminologists. Over 120 professional associations and training institutions are affiliated to FIT, representing more than 80,000 practitioners in 60 countries. The goal of the Federation is to promote professionalism in the disciplines it represents; it constantly seeks to improve conditions for the profession everywhere, and to uphold translators', interpreters' and terminologists' rights and freedom of expression.

Every three years, FIT invites the industry to an international congress. Following successful events in Shanghai in 2008 and Sun Francisco in 2011, Germany's Federal Association of Interpreters and Translators (BDÜ-Bundesverband der Dolmetscher und übersetzer e. V.) is delighted to be hosting the professional World, Congress in Berlin as the organiser of the XXth FIT World Congress, scheduled for 4 – 6 August, 2014.

Around the theme "Man vs. Machine—The Future of Translators, Interpreters and Terminologists". . .

What form will the work of translators, interpreters and terminologists take in the future? What challenges will they face? How will international market demands affect their services? How will individual national markets change?

All those interested in these questions are invited to submit proposals for presentations, workshops and panel discussions dealing with the following topics by 31 July, 2013.

● Translators, interpreters and terminologists-careers demanding a diverse range of expertise. . .

● How translation and interpreting contribute to safeguarding human rights. . .

● Professional practices and the rights of translators, interpreters and terminologists. . .

● Teaching and research in the field of translation, interpreting and terminology. . .

If you would like to share and present your knowledge and experience, please submit an abstract of up to 1,000 characters on the website www. fit2014. org by 31 July, 2013.

For more information, e-mail us at info@ fit2014. org.

Chinese Version

第 20 届世界翻译大会

2014 年 8 月 4 - 6 日在柏林举办

论文征集

国际翻译家联盟是口笔译工作者和术语学家的国际联合组织，拥有遍及 60 个国家的 120 余个专业协会和培训机构，代表全球 8 万余名翻译工作者的利益。其宗旨是推动建立翻译行业标准，不断改善全世界翻译行业状况，维护口笔译工作者和术语学家的权利和表达自由。

世界翻译大会每三年举办一次。继 2008 年第 18 届、2011 年第 19 届世界翻译大会分别在中国上海、美国旧金山成功举办之后，德国联邦翻译协会很高兴于 2014 年 8 月 4 - 6 日在柏林承办第 20 届世界翻译大会。

本届大会的主题是"人工翻译与机器翻译——翻译工作者与术语学家的未来"……

翻译工作者和术语学家的未来工作形式是什么？他们会面临什么样的挑战？国际翻译市场需求如何会影响其职业？各个国家的翻译市场将如何变化？

欢迎对这些问题感兴趣的人士提交与下列主题相关的提案，用于会议宣讲、研讨和小组交流，截止日期是 2013 年 7 月 31 日。

● 口笔译工作者与术语学家须具备多领域的各项专长……

● 口笔译在人权维护领域的贡献……

● 口笔译工作者与术语学家的职业实践与权利……

● 口笔译与术语领域的教研工作……

如果您想与大家分享自己的翻译知识和经验，请在 www. fit2014. org 网站提交不超过 1000 字的摘要，截止日期是 2013 年 7 月 31 日。

……

欲了解更多信息，请邮件联系 info@ fit2014. org.

Translation Practices

Translate the following into Chinese/English.

1. INSTRUCTIONS FOR AUTHORS

Selection of papers for presentation and inclusion in the digest will be made on the basis of abstracts submitted by intending authors. Abstracts and any supporting figures must be confined to a single A4 or 210mm×297mm page.

The letter accompanying the abstract must include the principal author's complete mailing address and fax number. All abstracts must be received by 12 April, 2013.

Forward abstracts to the Technical Program Chairman: (omitted)

Following review of abstracts by the Technical Committee authors will be advised by 16 May, 2013 whether their papers have been accepted or not. All papers must be in English.

Complete papers of length up to 4 pages, will be sought at that stage and must be received by 8 August 2013. The digest will be prepared directly from photo-ready materials submitted by authors and be provided to Conference attendees.

GENERAL ENQUIRIES

For general enquiries concerning the 2013 ASIA-PACIFIC LANGUAGE & CULTURE CONFERENCE direct enquiries to...

2. 本刊只接受全部用英文写成的稿件，截稿日期为 2016 年 12 月 31 日。来稿在 5000 单词左右为宜。论文必须另页附 200 字以内中文摘要、100 词以内英文摘要和不少于 3 个的关键词。正文格式应符合以下要求：1）英文 12 磅字体；2）双倍行距；3）左右两边空白各不少于 3.5 厘米；4）单面打印；5）段落第一行行首缩进四个字符；6）加入页码；7）文内引语和参考书目采用美国心理学学会（APA）的论文格式。

参考文献

［1］陈宏薇. 汉英翻译基础［M］. 上海：上海外语教育出版社，1998.

［2］陈文伯. 译艺——英汉汉英双向笔译［M］. 北京：世界知识出版社，2004.

［3］胡庚申. 文献阅读与翻译［M］. 北京：高等教育出版社，2003.

［4］林煌天. 中国翻译词典［M］. 武汉：湖北教育出版社，1997.

［5］刘宓庆. 新编汉英对比与翻译［M］. 北京：中国对外翻译出版公司，2006.

［6］申雨平，等. 实用汉英翻译教程［M］. 北京：外语教学与研究出版社，2002.

［7］宋天锡，等. 翻译新概念：英汉互译实用教程［M］. 北京：国防工业出版社，2000.

［8］张培基，等. 英汉翻译教程［M］. 上海：上海外语教育出版社，1986.

［9］Eugene A. Nida. *Language and Culture Contexts in Translating*［M］. Shanghai：Shanghai Foreign Language Education Press，2001.

［10］Munday Jeremy. *Introducing Translation Studies*［M］. London & New York：Routledge，2001.